Book of Magic

Book of Magic

Hugh Nightingale

p

This is a Parragon Book

First published in 2005

Parragon
Queen Street House
4 Queen Street
Bath BA1 1HE, UK

Designed, produced and packaged by Stonecastle Graphics Limited

Text and magic by Hugh Nightingale
Photography by Roddy Paine
Designed by Sue Pressley and Paul Turner
Artwork by Bill Donohoe
Edited by Gillian Haslam
Cover by Kit Rocket

ISBN 1-40545-284-6

Printed in China

About the author

Hugh Nightingale is a full-time professional magician,
entertaining audiences at various functions, from
corporate events to birthday parties and from society
dinners to street magic, both in close-up and in cabaret.
Hugh performs mainly in the UK and Europe and has
won awards for his magic. This is his second book on
magic for the aspiring newcomer. He also writes in the
magic press and has appeared on television several
times. Hugh is a member of The Magic Circle and in
2004 was elected into the Inner Magic Circle and
awarded the Gold Star, the highest degree in the society.
www.magico.co.uk

Disclaimer

Magic and card tricks are fun and this book will provide many
hours of amusement for magicians of all ages. Safety is very
important – young children should always be supervised by a
responsible adult when performing tricks involving sharp objects
or scissors. Always read the instructions carefully.
The publishers and their agents cannot accept liability for loss,
damage or injury however caused.

Contents

The Wonderful World of Magic

ONE DAY I came across an old magic book. At about the same time my son was to have his friends around for his fourth birthday party. 'I know,' I thought, 'I'll put on a magic show for them.' That was over 15 years ago and I have been bitten by the magic bug ever since. I am now a full-time professional magician and I still enjoy it as much as the day that I started. I do hope that this bug bites you as well and that you will have as much fun with magic as I have had.

Hugh Nightingale

The Ancient Art of Magic

The art of magic has certainly been practised since the time of the Pharaohs and probably for much, much longer. A hieroglyphic drawing found in one of the Pyramids in Egypt appears to depict a magician doing a trick with cups and balls. British magician Paul Daniels features a contemporary version of that trick in his show to this day, several thousands of years later, and it is still amazing. See page 84 for 'Tea Party' – our interpretation of this historic trick.

A magician of yesteryear 'conjures' up a spirit.

In his book *The Discoverie Of Witchcraft*, published in 1584, Reginald Scot documented many of the secrets of the magician in an attempt to prevent the persecution of several so-called witches. He was able to reveal that sleight of hand had been used rather than diabolic powers.

Much of the magic of ancient times was centred on spirits, death and gory subjects like decapitation. Summoning ghosts was always good for audience reaction in the eighteenth century. 'Magic lanterns' secretly projected spooky images – phantasmagoria – onto clouds of smoke or glass reflectors. Itinerant jugglers and magicians, together with musicians, acrobats and storytellers, travelled far and wide to country fairs and markets performing tricks such as 'The cups and balls' and 'Magic bags' with a seemingly inexhaustible supply of eggs, coins and cards – and even live fowl.

The nineteenth century saw a rise in the number of theatres, so magic shows gained great popularity in the world of vaudeville, while improved travel opportunities saw magic acts moving about the globe to and from America, Australia and the Far East.

Magic took off in a grand style in the early twentieth century, with the popularity of music halls. Names such as T. Nelson Downs –

King of Koins, Howard Thurston – King of Cards, Horace Goldin and his illusions and Chung Ling Soo with his Oriental Act attracted big audiences. The latter, whose real name was William Robinson, performed a wonderful act dressed as a Mandarin. One of his special tricks was very complicated and involved catching a bullet, but unfortunately one day it went tragically wrong and he was killed. Don't try that one at home!

The Father of Modern Magic

Jean Eugène Robert-Houdin (1805-1871) is often described as the 'father of modern magic'. He was one of the first to move away from dressing in Oriental robes or playing the part of the evil sorcerer. He performed in full evening dress, as do many magicians today. He also took full advantage of such modern inventions as electricity, which was relatively unknown at the time.

One of the illusions he performed was 'The Light and Heavy Chest'. Audience members were invited up on stage and asked to pick up a small wooden chest. Try as they might, none could move it and yet Robert-Houdin could always lift it with his little finger. Little did they know that the chest had a steel base and that hidden in the stage floor was an electromagnet controlled from the wings.

The Handcuff King

Harry Houdini (1874-1926) is best remembered for his remarkable escapology but he was also a master magician with coins and cards. He made dramatic escapes from chains, handcuffs, prison cells and even locked milk churns that were full of water. The secret of undoing the locks was amazing enough but perhaps he had hidden lock picks about his person. He had studied the art of the locksmith, which gives us a clue! How he managed to hold his breath for so long was even more

Robert-Houdin on stage with one of his automated illusions.

incredible. He could hardly hide an aqualung up his sleeve – especially when he was only wearing a pair of shorts! The secret was that he had trained himself to hold his breath for a long time and, when doing such stunts as being buried alive, to control his breathing and to use only slow and shallow breaths. He became known as The Handcuff King.

Houdini was a master of showmanship and could turn a clever but relatively minor stunt into a full evening's performance for an audience of thousands. A famous magic trick of his was Metamorphosis. He magically swapped places with his assistant who was locked and tied in a wooden trunk and managed it in only a few seconds. This is a trick that is still performed today but which has been taken to a whole new level. Today, The Pendragons basically do the same trick, but the swap happens in a fraction of a second and Charlotte Pendragon does a costume change as well! You may have seen this on television. It's unbelievable.

Harry Houdini photographed in chains prior to performing one of his breathtaking escapes.

'Impossible' Tricks

John Neville Maskelyne (1839-1917) trained as a watchmaker, which presumably gave him a thorough grounding in the art of precision manufacture. He was particularly well known for his mechanical automata. Probably the most famous was Psycho, a large 'doll' in Oriental dress that could move its arms and hands and play cards with onlookers. Not only could it handle the cards, which was incredible enough, it would also invariably win. Don't forget that 'radio control' had not been invented then.

Maskelyne was also famous for a box escape that seemed so impossible that he offered a reward to anyone who could discover the secret. Basically a committee from the audience inspected a large box equipped with ropes, chains and locks and proceeded to incarcerate his assistant within. The box was then put into a curtained cabinet. After a time the assistant emerged from the cabinet and yet the box was still found to be securely locked. The secret? There was another assistant hidden inside the curtained cabinet who undid the box. They both relocked and retied the box before the second assistant hid himself again while the first emerged triumphant. Just another form of misdirection. Everyone was so busy inspecting the box that no one checked the cabinet.

In 1873 Maskelyne organized a Theatre of Magic with George A. Cooke and later in 1904 he teamed up with the legendary magician David Devant. Two outstanding names in the history of magic were linked.

Poster advertising performances by Maskelyne and Cooke at the Egyptian Hall, London, c.1885.

Perform Your Own Box Escape Trick

Why not try an easy escapology trick yourself? You won't need a special cabinet or stage, just a large cardboard box, some rope and a scarf.

Ask your friends to bind your wrists securely and then tie you into the box. Then, as the London fog extends its wispy fingers across the icy waters of the River Thames, they drop you off London Bridge into the murky depths... Oops, I think I might have left the words 'pretend to' out of the last sentence.

Use your imagination and tell a story to set the scene for your audience. But before you attempt any escape trick, read the safety tips below and be sure that everything is absolutely safe. Here, my assistant Lucy performs the box escape while I act as her assistant from the audience.

Performance notes

• If you are pretending to hold your breath, even though you are only performing on the living room carpet, then ask the audience to count out loud.
• Also, take a tip from Houdini: if you say that you can hold your breath for 45 seconds, delay your escape until the very last second to build up the tension (even if you could have easily escaped after 10 seconds). It's called showmanship!

Safety tips

• Never attempt escapology in any situation that is dangerous or could potentially become so. Professional escapologists train for many years and, even so, tragic accidents can occur. Instead build up a dramatic element of danger by clever story telling and acting. Play on the imaginations of your audience.
• Even if everything seems safe, always have a reliable friend standing by just in case you really do get stuck – even when rehearsing.

Ask someone to tie the scarf around your wrists as shown and secure it with several knots. Note how you hold your wrists edge to edge. This will give you a little slack later, when you rotate them, which will make the escape easier.

The long rope is passed around the scarf, through the circle of your arms and out through a small hole low down in the front of the box. This will cause you to bend down and you can pretend that this will hold your head below the 'water'. The audience can start to 'count down' as the ropes around the sides of the box are secured.

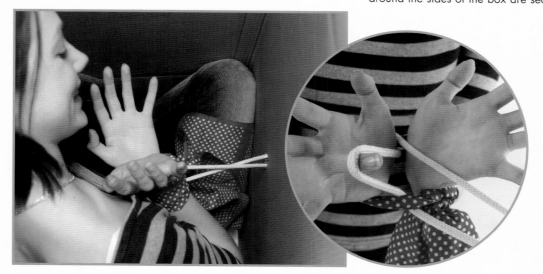

Unknown to the audience you keep your wrists close to your body rather than near the side of the box. This will also give you the slack you need for your escape.

Inside the box, you work to loosen the rope between your wrists – through the loop of the scarf – to create some slack (see inset above right). This will enable you to pass one of your hands through the loop of rope that you have made.

The rope will now come free of your wrists and you can stand up in triumph. You will probably find that you can now also slip your wrists out of the scarf.

Amazing Illusions

David Devant (1868-1941) was 'the greatest of English magicians' and first president of *The Magic Circle*. He became interested in magic as a young boy and was sacked from his job at the age of 14 for practising conjuring tricks at work. (So be warned – don't get caught!) He performed many illusions as well as excellent sleight of hand tricks. He became world-famous for his amazing stunts involving the disappearance of people, many of which have rarely been attempted since.

His inventive shows included the 'Magic Kettle' from which he poured any drink called for by the audience, the 'Disappearing Donkey' and 'The Moth and the Flame'. In the latter, a girl in a moth costume approached a candle that Devant was holding. As she got near to it she stopped and hid her face from the candle with her wings. Then, as Devant approached her, she disappeared. The secret? Apparently, as she closed her wings, she managed to slip through a trapdoor beneath her that had a platform lift below it. All this happened in the fraction of a second during which Devant stepped in front of her.

Devant continues to inspire magicians to this day. There is a story of how he was once speaking to a young amateur magician. 'How many tricks can you do?' he asked 'Oh, at least forty' said the boy. 'Really,' he said, 'when I was your age I could do only six … but I could do them all perfectly.' A lesson to us all, I believe.

Famous American magician Harry Blackstone with a young woman who is carefully positioned on a machine and apparently being sawn in half.

Famous Tricks

One of the most famous tricks of all time must be 'Sawing A Lady In Half' and one of the first and foremost inventors of this effect was P. T. Selbit (1879-1938). This illusion has been performed in many forms ever since – you may have seen David Copperfield's recent version on television. In earlier times this had a great effect on audiences and the tension was often heightened by having doctors, and even morticians, on standby in the theatre.

The Magic Circle

On a summer's day in 1905, 23 amateur and professional magicians gathered together in London with the intention of forming a magic club. The result was the founding of *The Magic Circle*.

The Magic Circle remains the most prestigious society in the world of magic and illusion. It has an international membership of around 1500 magicians, all dedicated to promoting and advancing the art of magic, which is as popular today as it was when the famous club was formed.

In 1998 *The Magic Circle* realized a long-held ambition when it opened its own purpose-built headquarters in Euston, London.

Here, in addition to a superb fully equipped theatre, it has libraries, a splendid museum and a vast collection of posters and memorabilia relating to the history of mystery. The clubrooms are regular meeting places for leading magicians, and in this unique setting *The Magic Circle* also presents special events where visitors can experience the wonderful atmosphere and be entertained by top magicians, sometimes including your author.

The words '*Indocilis Privata Loqui*', roughly translated, mean 'not apt to disclose secrets' and this soon became the motto of *The Magic Circle* and to this day appears on its logo.

www.TheMagicCircle.co.uk

Modern-Day Magic

The advent of television, although blamed for the demise of the music halls, brought magic shows into almost every home and made household names of magicians such as David Nixon – gentleman of magic, Tommy Cooper – funny man of magic, Robert Harbin – inventive genius of magic, Ali Bongo – the Shriek of Araby, David Berglas – expert on Mind Magic and, of course, Paul Daniels whose name became synonymous with magic itself.

The United States has always performed magic on a grand scale with acts like David Copperfield who can vanish anything from jet planes to the Statue of Liberty, Siegfried and Roy with their spectacular Las Vegas Show, Penn and Teller's outrageous magic and Lance Burton with his suave manipulations and doves. Doug Henning appeared on the scene with The Magic Show on Broadway and performed wearing jeans. Unheard of until then, he was one of the first 'cool' magicians. David Blaine has now taken 'cool' to a whole new level – especially when encased in a block of ice!

This is, of course, only a snippet of magic's rich history but if you search the libraries and the Internet, you will be able to discover much more. Reading about the greats and even the not-so-greats of magic will undoubtedly enrich and inspire your performance.

Robert Harbin of The Maskelyne and Devant Company photographed in 1965 performing his illusion 'Zig-Zag Lady', assisted by a member of the audience.

American magician David Blaine in his transparent box near Tower Bridge, London in September 2003. He spent 44 days suspended in the box without food.

Classic Illusions

Illusions continue to astonish and amaze us to this day, deceiving audiences into believing that they are seeing almost supernatural occurrences. For many, part of the fun in watching them is to attempt to work out the 'secret' and as a student of magic you probably want to do the same. I do not want to spoil your fun by simply giving you the answers, but here are some possible methods that could be used for three famous illusions.

Naturally, I can only offer you these possible explanations following consultation with *The Magic Circle* at the highest level. There are, of course, many other variations and you will, I am sure, think of ways in which these could be improved to make them even more convincing. The first, 'The Lady Vanishes', is an illusion that you could easily perform for a stage production or pantomime without having to construct any special equipment.

The Lady Vanishes

MOST MAGICIANS will tell you that the question that they are most often asked after 'How did you do that?' is 'Can you make my wife (or husband) disappear?' Well, they think it's funny! Anyway, here is a method for making your fellow conspirator vanish from the stage.

Our magician has helped this young lady on to a table and he holds a large flag. The audience can see under the table so they know that there cannot be a trapdoor there.

He momentarily lifts the flag in front of her... and she's gone!

The audience can see right through the table legs to the curtain behind. She has simply vanished. But where?

Where did she go?

As you can now see, there is a small curtain hanging down behind the table. This exactly matches the backcloth curtain so that from the audience's position it appears that they can only see the backcloth.

Curtain hanging from back of table top

Tips

• Speed and timing are of the essence here in order to catch the audience off guard. Many magicians use music in their illusions in order to keep to the beat.

• To get up to speed, illusionists rehearse, rehearse, and then rehearse ten times more!

• The assistant must jump lightly down at the exact split second that the flag is at its highest point in front of her.

Sawing a Lady in Half

YOU WILL recall how P.T. Selbit invented an illusion in which his assistant was sawn in half. This is one of the most famous tricks of all time. Many methods of performing it have been developed over the years and here is one. The *modus operandi* is self-explanatory from the illustrations.

Tips

- For a scarier effect the assistant can let out a scream as the saw 'apparently' penetrates her body.
- Assistants for an effect like this need to be physically fit, supple and to train very hard. Often dancers, they are almost contortionists and certainly not claustrophobic!
- The secret assistant must wear identical shoes.
- The apparatus should be custom-made by a specialist propmaker or engineer.

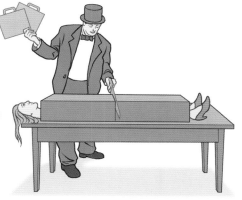

The magician introduces his assistant and helps her into a box. 'Ladies and Gentlemen, I would like to introduce you all to my sister. She is going to help me with my next trick by having a rest in this box.'

He then appears to saw right through her body and inserts two 'blades' into the cut. 'I do hope you are feeling comfortable. I would hate you to feel sore (saw – groan!) so just relax and try not to feel a blade – oops, I meant afraid.'

'Oh, I forgot to mention,' as he separates the two parts, 'that she is actually my HALF-sister.' (More groans!) The audience can see right through the middle of her body. Obviously he then puts her back together again and they both stand for their applause.

The secret is revealed

A hidden assistant hides in a compartment in the table before the act begins. As the magician goes through the process of helping his 'sister' into the box, the hidden assistant puts her feet out through the footholes in the end of the box. For the restoration, the reverse procedure is followed. Only the secret assistant misses out on the applause!

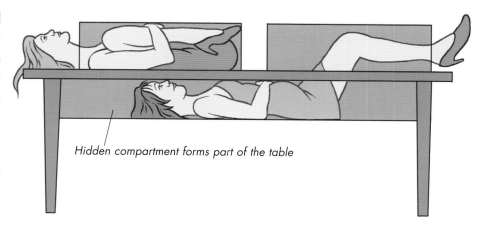

Hidden compartment forms part of the table

Levitating Lady

YOU MAY be aware of a world-famous illusion performed by David Copperfield where he flies around the stage – sometimes even taking a member of the audience up with him in his arms. The following trick may not be quite in that league but it should get you thinking. To make even a small object (like a ring or a pencil) appear to float in the air is a good illusion, but to make another human being levitate above the ground is miles better. So how can our magician make this young lady hover weightlessly above the stage?

The magician introduces his assistant and also shows the audience a stool, which he carries to centre stage. The fact that he carries it on seems to prove its innocence.

He makes her comfortable on the stool and stands back to weave his magic spell. As he has already walked behind the stool, the audience knows there is no special attachment at the back.

Slowly he draws the stool out from under her and, with his wand, 'proves' there is no hidden prop supporting her. He also waves his wand above her to show there are no strings attached.

So how is it done?

While the magician helps the lady onto the stool, he also surreptitiously guides a special steel pole into a socket on an extra false seat which rests on top of the real seat.

Look at this exposed side view and you will see the monkey business is all backstage! From behind the curtain a pole is pushed through a gap in the curtain by a burly stagehand. Using trestles he can offer unseen support to the 'floating' lady assistant.

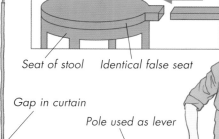

Seat of stool   Identical false seat

Gap in curtain

Pole used as lever

Trestles

Tips

• There must be marks on the stage floor so that the magician can position the stool in exactly the right place.

• Sometimes the magician will act as if he has hypnotized his assistant and it is this that makes her appear lighter than air.

• Note how the assistant's long skirt hides any evidence of the false seat.

• For safety, this apparatus must be specially constructed to the correct strengths and tolerances.

Polishing Your Performance

ONCE YOU have read this book you will know many of the magician's techniques. Practise every day until you know the procedures like the back of your hand. Will you then be a magician? Well, nearly.

Magic is more than just a method, it is an art. Your props and techniques are the instruments with which you will perform, the brushes with which you will paint your picture in the minds of your audience. Know them well. Wear them comfortably. Tailor them until they fit your personality, discard those that do not. If you bought a new outfit you might ask a trusted friend, 'How does it look?' Do the same thing with a new routine. Your techniques may be without fault but you will need a good friend to tell you to drop a trick that does not suit you and to concentrate on others that do. Here are some useful performance tips for aspiring magicians:

Finding Your Own Style

• You may want to perform in a smart dinner jacket or evening dress with bright and shiny props, or dress casually and use everyday objects like a rolled-up newspaper and a few coins. You choose, but either way there is no excuse for scruffiness. Practise so that you never have to fumble or act clumsily.

• Always make quite clear what you are doing, but without saying what you are about to do. After all, something may go wrong and you may have to change what you were about to do! It is better if the audience do not realize. Write out your 'patter'. Make it as bright as possible, adding humour whenever you can, and be prepared with extra anecdotes if you have to cover some technical problem or delay.

• Avoid dull descriptions: 'Now I will take a pack of cards, now I will shuffle the cards, now I will have a card chosen, now I will have that card replaced in the pack, now I will find … now I will find I have to wake up my audience as they have fallen asleep thanks to my boring patter'. If you do not want to speak, perform silent magic and employ music or mime.

• When practising your tricks, do it in front of a mirror occasionally to study every move as well as the position of your hands and your body. Discover where it is best for you to stand in relation to the audience. Check all your 'angles' so that no one can spot something that they are not supposed to see.

• Don't be disappointed by the simplicity of a trick. If the method is simple, you will be able to put much more showmanship into it.

• Always be on the alert to improve the finer points of your tricks in every possible way, even if you have been performing the same trick for 15 years – I speak for myself as well here. Enjoy your own performance and audiences will enjoy watching it. Always leave them wanting more so that, with luck, they may ask you to perform again on another occasion.

Avoiding Exposure

• Often you will be begged to 'do it again'. Never be persuaded, because if you do the same thing twice, the secret may well be spotted. Pass the matter off by moving on to a fresh trick or claim that you wish you could do it again but unfortunately magician's laws forbid it.

• Every time there is some move to be concealed, try to 'misdirect' the audience. This can be done in many ways by saying something, making eye contact or doing something that will transfer their attention elsewhere.

• Never let an audience see any of your preparations. If you think that there might be an opportunity to perform at a party or dinner, pop to the bathroom for a minute to check that your 'props' are all set. It looks really bad if, when asked to do a trick, you have to turn your back to 'get ready'.

• Beware of mirrors or people standing behind you. You should make every effort never to expose your magic secrets either by poor performance or by telling all – even though you will be pressured to do so by many a spectator.

Easy Magic

Vanishing a Pencil

I MPROMPTU VANISH or 'ear today, gone tomorrow' is a really fun vanish that I often use. You can use it for vanishing many pencil-shaped objects but the bonus is that, while you are vanishing the pencil or whatever, you do a second vanish right in front of your spectator.

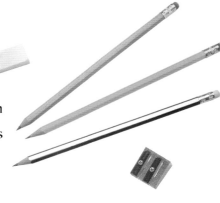

Because you use an ordinary object like a pen or pencil this can be done impromptu so it is a good one for the office or school.

State that you will vanish an object, in our case an eraser, by tapping it three times with your pencil. It will vanish on the third tap. Looking at the photographs you will see that just before the third tap you actually slide the pencil behind your ear. Your spectator will be concentrating so hard on the eraser, in the hope of seeing how it will disappear, that they will not see you leave the pencil behind your ear at all. In fact, after a couple of seconds you will have to turn yourself side-on to them and indicate that they must look behind your ear.

Now for the really sneaky bit. While they look at your ear and chuckle at how easily they were fooled, you slip the eraser into your pocket. This move is hidden by your body.

Immediately return your hand, now empty, to where it was. You say something like 'Only joking' and strike the pencil down on to your hand one more time. The spectator's eyes will follow the movement of the pencil and will be astounded to see that as it hits your hand, the eraser really has gone!

Practice tip

• The moves are not difficult but the timing is very important. Practise by hitting your hand with a pencil three times. Then try leaving the pencil behind your ear on the third beat. The timing should be the same whether you leave it behind or not. If you have to fiddle around to get it to stay behind your ear, the audience might easily notice what you are up to.

Show the eraser and explain how you will hit it three times. Strike the eraser twice.

On the third time leave the pencil behind your ear.

Turn your body away from your audience and point to your ear while you slip the eraser into your pocket. Here we have exaggerated the move!

Take the pencil from behind your ear and strike towards your hand again. Your audience does not realize that your hand is already empty.

The eraser has vanished!

Rip-Off

THIS IS a real quickie which takes just a few seconds to set up. The effect is that you show your friends your new necklace. So they can have a closer look, you offer to take it off, but you are a magician so why bother to undo it? Just pull the whole thing through your neck!

Obviously anybody could do this trick by undergoing many hours of painful neurosurgery and ending up with their head held in place by a Frankenstein bolt. There is a slightly easier way.

Our magician is wearing a leather necklace around his neck.

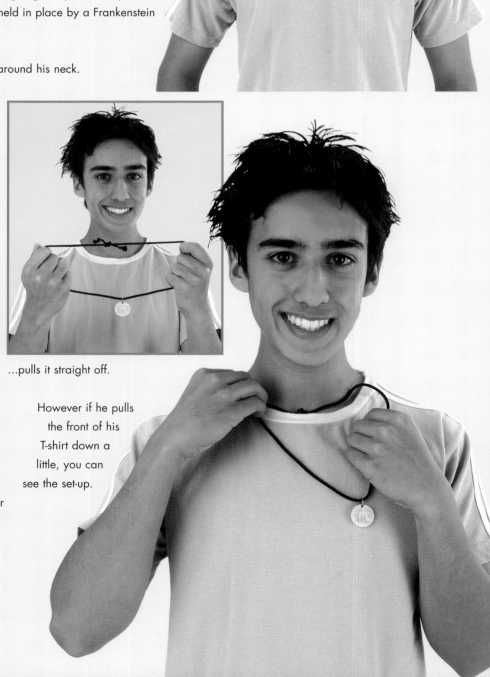

He takes hold and...   ...pulls it straight off.

Tips

• This type of leather necklace will stay in place for some time after setting up.

• Also this depends upon the weight of the T-shirt holding it in place. So a little while before you want to try this, pop out of sight or into the bathroom for a moment to get ready.

• Don't try it with a thin white T-shirt – everyone will be able to see through it and the secret will be revealed.

Have fun with this!

However if he pulls the front of his T-shirt down a little, you can see the set-up.

A Couple of 'Handy' Illusions

WHEN PEOPLE find out that you are a magician they may well ask you one of two questions: 'Can you make my wife (or husband) disappear?' or 'Can you saw me in half?' With the first, it is polite to fall about laughing at their joke, as they will not realize that you have heard it 17 times already that day. With the second, you can use it as a perfect introduction to this trick or optical illusion.

Handy Illusion 1

Reply by stating that one of the nastiest cuts is a paper cut to the hand. However, you are going to use a piece of paper to create a hole through their hand that will not hurt and will instantly heal itself.

Roll the paper into a tube.

Ask them to look through the tube as if it were a telescope.

Now they must hold their other hand out flat, with its edge against the tube, near the end furthest from themselves.

Now ask them to open both eyes. To their surprise they will see a hole right through the middle of their hand.

Handy Illusion 2

Another fun optical illusion allows you to state that a magician need never go hungry as he can always make a cocktail sausage appear.

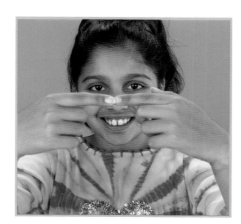

Ask a member of the audience to touch their two fingers together about 30cm (12in) in front of their face as shown. Can they see anything odd? Now ask them to look past their fingers at you.

They will appear to see what looks like a small sausage between their fingers. Reach forward, 'grab' it from them and pretend to stuff something into your mouth and eat it.

Ask them to look back at their fingers. The sausage will have gone!

Tip

• Naturally, you will have to try these two on yourself to fully appreciate the effects.

Magnetic Hands

ONE OF THE golden rules of magic is never repeat a trick. People will beg, flatter and threaten (!) you to try and persuade you to do so, but don't. Tell them it is against the rules of your magic society, show them something else, run away to sea, anything, but do not repeat the trick. When they ask, it usually means that they think they might know how it is done, they just need to see it one more time to confirm that they are right.

Now do you see why you must not repeat a trick?

Having said that, here is a trick that you can repeat not once but twice. OK, it appears to break the rule but, in fact, although you do the effect three times, each is by a different method. You are, in fact, showing them three different tricks but they seem the same.

This is an easy impromptu trick that is particularly well suited to a school or college environment. People have heard of static electricity. A rubbed balloon sticks to the wall or a shred of paper clings to your comb, but how about something solid like a pencil, a ruler or even a small book clinging eerily to your hand.

Look at the audience view of each of these three tricks. Don't they look convincing?

Now look at a 'behind the scenes' view of each.

Does any more need to be said?

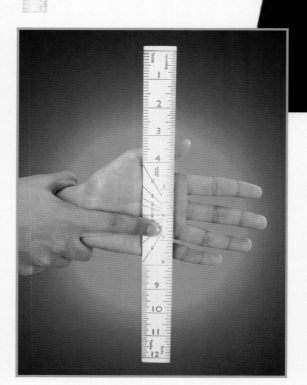

Tip

• It is a very good idea to learn more than one method for a magic effect. For instance, if you can vanish a coin in two different ways, then, when someone says, 'Do that again', you can. They will be looking to see if they can spot the first method. When you use an alternative method, they will be totally flummoxed.

Notes

• The extra ruler is up your sleeve, held by your watchstrap. It should be in place before you start but only secretly slid out when required for the last effect.

• You will need to practise interlocking your fingers to achieve the second effect. Looking from the audience's point of view, you do not notice that a finger is 'missing'. In fact, when you try it, you will probably confuse yourself!

Mind Signals

A VERY EASY mind-reading trick. Three objects are placed in a row. You, our psychic sorcerer, leave the room while the audience decide upon one object. When you return, you ask the whole audience to think hard about that object and, after you have apparently tuned in to their thoughts, you reveal which it is. Now this one is very simple, yes, but played well, it is very, very deceptive.

Place three objects in a row before you.

The mystery?

You have a secret helper in the audience. You just pre-arrange some clandestine signals that no one else in the audience will notice.

For instance, if your helper has his left hand in his pocket, it is the object on the left-hand side. If it is his right hand, then it is the one on the right-hand side. No hands in pockets mean it is the one in the middle. Or, if sitting with legs crossed, then left leg on top, right leg on top or uncrossed legs could be the signals. Or hands crossed on his lap, or which hand is on the arm of the chair, or in which hand he is holding his handkerchief.

The codes are endless and I would advise you not to use the same code more than once. Certainly never use the same code more than twice or someone could easily spot it and your future as the world's greatest mind-reading team will be very short-lived indeed. The audience will definitely want you to repeat this one. Normally I say never repeat a trick but here you will have to, in order to prove that it was not just a coincidence. That is why, when you repeat the trick, you alter your signal code.

The accomplice gives the magician the signal, unseen by the rest of the audience around him.

Acting like a real mind reader – if there are such people – the magician reveals the correct object.

Tips

• Decide on a sequence of codes with your helper. If you are going to do the trick four times, you might do pocket, leg, hands, handkerchief as the series. As long as you both know this, you will not get confused.

• Since you will be facing one another, decide whether you mean *his* right and left or yours. Rather important, this one!

• Do not walk in and stare at your accomplice. That would give the secret away. Just glance around the room and pick up the signal as your eyes take in the whole audience.

• Do not use an active signal, such as him tugging his ear or rubbing his shoulder. They are too easy for others to spot and will give you both away. A cough, as you mention the right object, has been tried before and was a famous failure!

Three Glass Challenge

Here you actually demonstrate how the trick is performed and then challenge a participant to have a go, but he cannot repeat your success.

The challenge

To turn the glasses over, two at a time, and finish with all the glasses mouth upwards. It must be done in exactly three moves.

Begin by showing three glasses. Two one way up, one the other.

Turn over the two on your left.

Now cross your arms over and turn over the glasses at each end.

Finally turn over the two glasses on your left again.

And all three will be the right way up.

Now turn the middle glass downwards and challenge someone else to try.

Did you spot it?

At first glance it looks like you have reset the glasses to the starting position but if you look closely at the photos you will see the difference. It is very unlikely that anyone will notice this and they will not be able to solve the challenge from this starting point. By crossing you arms and doing the moves very quickly, your audience will be unable to follow exactly what you do.

Key to the Wizard's Den

Y OU CLAIM to have a key that used to belong to your great, great, great, great, great, great grandfather who was a wizard. Legend has that if it is placed on the hand of someone who has inherited the wizard's powers, the key will turn by itself to unlock the 'force'.

Gather your friends around into a magic circle. One by one you place the key on their hands. The room falls quiet and a sudden chill causes a shiver to run down their spines. The key, though, lies perfectly still. Now, standing in the middle of the circle you place the key on your hand. The sky grows dark and a strange and unintelligible murmuring is heard to come from your lips. All eyes are fixed on your hand as slowly, very slowly, the key begins to turn all by itself.

Scary, huh? And if you happen to be good at telling ghost stories, this would be the perfect opportunity as you will be able to get everyone's imaginations working overtime.

So what do you need? Well, lots of acting to create a spooky atmosphere and an old-fashioned mortice lock key. Someone in the family might have an old one or you can often find them in junk shops.

How to make the key turn

Place the key so that the round handle part is not touching your palm while the key part is facing towards your thumb.

Simply tip your hand gently downwards, so slowly that no one can see it move.

No, even slower than that.

The key is really moving now, so don't giggle and break the spell.

You have the power.

Tips

• Basically, this just requires practising until you get the key to turn without it falling on the floor. Then practise some more until you can make it turn very slowly.

• It would add to the mystery and allure of this effect if you made a special box for your key. You could paint a small cardboard box black and line it with red velvet. Or how about going really Gothic and shaping it like a tiny coffin? Now, that would be spooky!

• Bigger and heavier keys look better and tend to turn more slowly and dramatically, so they are easier to use.

• Now you have learnt the right way to place it on your hand, remember when you put it on your friends' hands to make sure that you place it the wrong way. After all, you don't want them being able to do it by accident!

Transporter Pocket

'**B**EAM ME UP.' Wouldn't it be great to have your own private transporter room so that you could beam yourself to anywhere in the world? Well, I haven't quite mastered that myself yet, so let's start a little smaller. How about impressing your friends by invisibly transporting a napkin to a different part of the room?

Show them five differently coloured paper napkins and have one chosen.

Pull out your pocket to show that it is empty.

Scrunch up the napkin and then put it in your pocket.

Do a little 'hocus-pocus' and command the napkin to fly to the middle of a book on the shelf at the other end of the room.

Pull your pocket right out again. It's empty!

By now one of your friends will have fetched the book whether you wanted them to or not. Open the book and there is the napkin.

This is really easy for the absolute beginner in magic. You need five different colours of napkin – two of each colour. You hide one of each colour in five different places around the room where they are unlikely to be discovered by accident. In a vase, behind a picture – well, you know your room better than I do. I am sure that you can find five hiding places and do not forget where each is hidden. Do all this before your friends arrive.

The vanish?

Complicated sleight of hand? No. You simply push the scrunched up napkin into the top front corner of your pocket. It will stay hidden there even when you pull your pocket right out.

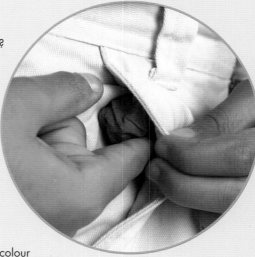

Tip

• If you only have one of each colour napkin, then sometimes you will find that they are two-ply or four-ply, so that you can split one into two. They will also then scrunch up smaller, which is useful.

Magic Changing Bag

MAN HAS always been fascinated by magically changing things – base metal into gold, plain paper into money notes, frogs into handsome princes. The last one can be a little tricky, but most small changes can appear to happen with this really simple, useful prop.

To make the magic bag

You will need three squares of felt. The centre one could be a tiny bit smaller than the outer two, so that the 'third' edge will not show.

Use craft glue around three edges, press flat, and allow to dry.

When in use, fold the top edges over slightly so that the double edge will not be seen. It is easy to unfold this and refold the other way during the course of the trick.

You can use all sorts of material to make your bag as exotic as you like. You could even line the compartments with black lining material, sew it all together and decorate with tassels. I have only used felt and glue – well, I'm a magician, not a seamstress!

The frog and the prince

Here's a simple routine to give you an idea of how to use your change bag. Once you have made one, you will think of hundreds of uses for it.

Show a picture of a frog to your audience. For extra dramatic effect you could draw or print it out in front of them.

(There is already a picture of a prince in the other compartment, but we don't know that, do we?)

Turn the edges of the bag over to show that it is empty inside.

Fold the picture of the frog and place it into the bag.

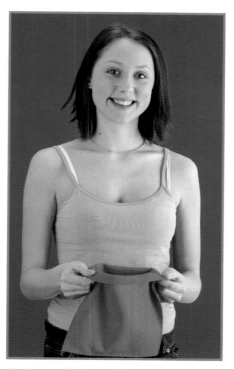

Shake it well down – this is your 'cover' for opening the other compartment.

Blow a kiss towards the bag. Male magicians might like to ask a young lady to do this.

Reach in, remove the picture, unfold it...

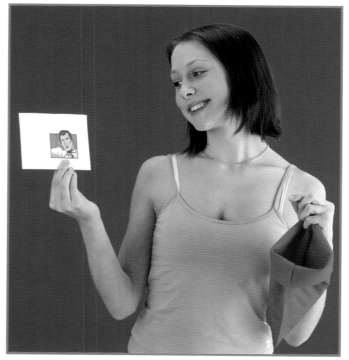

...and, of course, it is no longer a frog but a handsome prince!

You may now, of course, turn the bag inside out to show that it is empty again.

Tips
• Mark one side of your home-made Magic Changing Bag with a little stitch of white thread so that you will never forget which side is which.
• A really simple and cheap bag could be made from a couple of paper bags. Cut away one side of one of the bags and glue it to the other bag to make a divider. It won't last that long but it will work. I know, I've tried it and it is great for a one-off show.

Hanky Prank

THIS IS an easy method for vanishing all sorts of small objects. Little preparation is needed, as you only require one small rubber band and a silk scarf or large handkerchief.

We will use this to make someone's ring disappear. Oh, and I suppose that we had better make it come back as well.

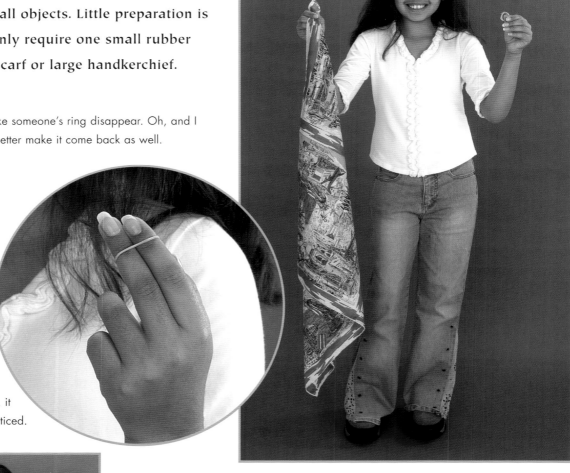

Preparation

Slip the small rubber band around the tips of your first and second fingers.

Don't be worried about people spotting this – with your hand held naturally at your side, it cannot be noticed.

Ask to borrow a ring as you spread the scarf over your hand.

A secret look under the scarf shows us that you should now get your thumb into the band as well.

Place the ring on top of the scarf as your fingers open out the band directly underneath and...

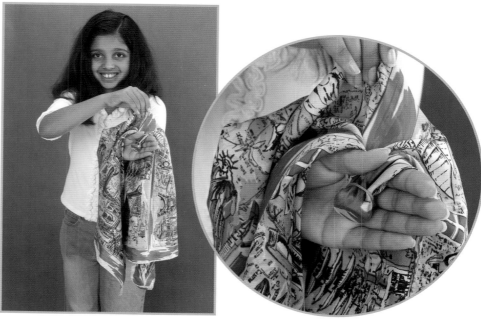

...give it a magic rub.

This ensures that the ring goes well into the band, which closes over it, as you slip your fingers out.

Now whip the scarf away with a flourish and stare at your empty hand.

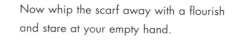

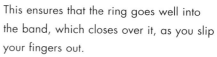

Before the lender of the ring calls their insurance company – reach into the folds of the scarf and magically recover the ring.

Tips

• After the vanish, looking at your empty hand is good misdirection. Do not look at the scarf.

• After you have found the ring again, keep the band on one finger or, even better, let it fall unseen to the floor. Then you can give back the ring and safely hand out the scarf in case anyone wants to inspect it.

The Magic Wand

A WAND can be a great help in your magic act, but unless it is made from the wood of a 3000-year-old yew tree planted adjacent to Merlin's grave, it is unlikely to create thunderbolts! However, it will misdirect your audience. If you are hiding (palming) something in your hand, then that hand will tend to look a lot more natural if it is also holding your magic wand. Furthermore, waving a wand will draw the audience's eyes away from something that you don't want them to see.

The effect

If you are going to use a wand – why not produce it with some magic and fun?

Opening a small purse, you take out a tiny wand with an air of disappointment. Your audience will laugh and you then share their amusement. Replacing it, you then remove a wand many times larger than the purse. With perhaps a little amazement on your own part, you now can push the wand back in and out of the purse. It is not a telescopic wand as you subsequently prove to your audience.

The first part requires no magic, but introduces the opportunity for some comedy and facial expression – making the audience laugh will help you to catch them completely off guard with what follows.

Construction notes

• The wand is made from painted dowelling.
• The fake end is made from white card rolled into a tube that can slide up and down on the wand.
• The purse simply has a slit or a seam undone at the bottom corner that is held nearest to your sleeve.
• You will need to wear a jacket or something with long sleeves to conceal the wand.

Tips

• For no apparent reason, acts or routines often seem to work exceptionally well when they consist of three parts. Here the tiny wand gag, the wand from sleeve and the sliding-end wand are a good example of this.
• This makes a great opening trick. If it is to be performed later in your act, then secure the wand up your sleeve using your watchstrap or a rubber band. You don't want the wand appearing too early!

Slowly pull the large wand through the slit in the prepared purse.

The hand holding the purse should look relaxed and natural.

Remove the wand with final theatrical flourish.

The large wand has been attached to your arm behind your watchstrap all the time.

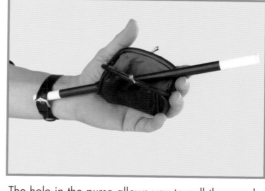

The hole in the purse allows you to pull the wand through to the amazement of your audience.

The third part of the effect is to push the wand in and out of the tiny purse.

Hold the fake white tip and slide it downwards as the wand is 'returned' to the purse. Most of the real wand is hidden behind your hand and arm.

If the audience was suspicious of your left sleeve after the previous part of the trick, they certainly will be baffled now. Easy!

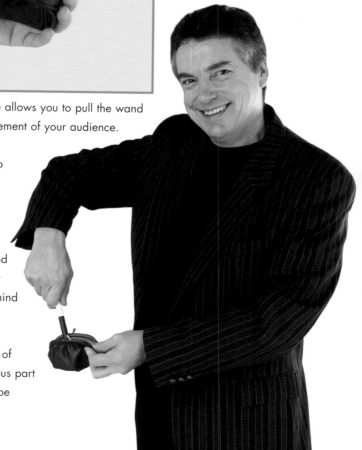
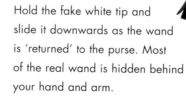

Penetrating Pencil

ALTHOUGH THIS book tells you time and time again not to repeat a trick, there is an exception – when the repeat uses an entirely different method.

Here are two methods for getting a pencil to pass through a handkerchief. They could be performed separately or as a pair.

Horizontal method

Lay the pencil on the handkerchief and fold it diagonally so that the pencil is trapped inside.

Tip

• Remember to stress to the audience that the pencil starts off trapped inside. This way they will appreciate the escape even more.

Roll up the handkerchief as shown.

When you unroll the handkerchief, the pencil has now escaped to the outside.

The secret. As you make the diagonal fold, make sure that the upper triangle is more than half of the handkerchief.

Then, as you reach the end of the rolling, allow only one corner to flip over. This will be the original shorter side.

As you begin to unroll, everything looks the same but in reality the top triangle of the handkerchief is the original lower triangle.

Vertical method

Drape a large handkerchief over your clenched fist.

Make a shallow well in the top with your finger.

Push the pencil into the well.

Then pull it right out through the bottom!

Tip
Put the handkerchief on your hand slightly unevenly, with more material at the front than at the back. This gives you more cover, thus making it easier for you and more deceptive for the audience.

What the audience doesn't see

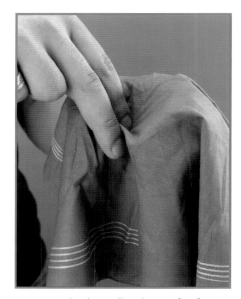

As you make the well with your forefinger, your second finger makes a crease in the material from the back.

When you apparently put the pencil in the well, you actually slide it behind the crease.

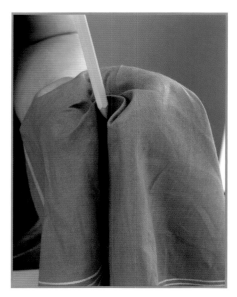

Try it and you will see how realistically the pencil seems to pass through the cloth.

Tadpole Tickling Trickery

THIS IS a good trick to entertain children, but adults will be just as baffled, because you are able to predict the exact place that a child will choose to tickle the tadpole. The tadpole refers to the shape that you make with your chosen objects. You can use all kinds of small items, such as matches, cards, sugar cubes, coins or cornflakes. But please don't use real tadpoles – they are so difficult to train! You can use any coins – large or small – but they should ideally be identical.

Tip
• Your helper can think of any number that is bigger than the number of coins in the tail but less than the total number of coins.

To begin, you will need about 30–40 coins.

Firstly, lay the coins out in the tadpole shape shown here. The 'eye' coins are just added for a bit of fun. The exact number is not important.

Introduce your tadpole and explain that he likes nothing more than being tickled on his back first and then, most of all, on his tummy. Your child helper is asked to think of a number between 10 and 30 (see tip above).

Then, starting at the end of the tail they count along the coins, up the tail and along the back. When they reach their chosen number, they can give him a little tickle on that coin.

Now, using the same number, they count back, missing out the tail, along to his tummy. When they reach their number, they should give him a big tickle on that coin.

'So where's the magic?' I hear you ask.

Turn over the tickled tummy coin and there is a sticker on the other side that says 'THIS ONE'. No other coins have stickers.

The secret? Following the instructions above they will always finish the same number away from where the 'tail' joins the 'body' as there are coins in the tail. If you wish to repeat it another time then make up the shape with a different number of coins in the tail, but don't make this obvious.

Bangle Wrangle

FLEXIBLE BANGLES are very popular with girls these days. Here is a stunt using one of these that seems impossible. All you need is some rope, a bangle and a jacket.

Ask someone to test a short length of cord or rope for you.

Tip

• When you ask someone to tie the rope, get them to concentrate on making several knots on each side rather than making the rope too tight around your wrist. We don't want the trick to be too difficult or your hands to shrivel and fall off!

Put your arms through the sleeves of a jacket or shirt the wrong way round, as shown above. Ask your volunteer to tie your wrists together with the cord.

Leave a bangle threaded on the middle of the cord. Ask your volunteer to check that the bangle is secure.

We will now remove the jacket for the photographs, so that you can discover the secret method

Squeeze one of your hands through the bangle. It will end up on your wrist next to the rope.

Now ease it over the wrist tie and further up your arm.

Now slide the bangle under the rope and off your wrist. Because the bangle is smooth and flexible, it will slip back through even if the rope is fairly tight. Now throw open the jacket to show your success. It's easy when you know how.

Bonus extra

To make the trick look even more impossible:
- Knot the bangle onto the middle of the rope first.
- To remove, loosen the knot into a loop and thread the bangle along the rope following the loop
  - As soon as it is out of the loop, proceed as above.

Let the jacket slide down over your wrists so that your hands are hidden. Now you will get the bangle off the rope without untying your wrists.

Your wrists have remained tied with the cord but the bangle has been removed. Your audience will be amazed.

Bandtastic

'**F**IFTEEN YEARS of practice has enabled me to do this amazing thing with a rubber band.' Well, that is how I often introduce this effect before I perform it. In fact if you set aside 15 minutes to learn the method, you should still have enough time left over to make yourself a sandwich!

The effect is that you seem to be able to make a rubber band jump from two of your fingers to two different ones at impossible speed. Surely such ability can only have been learned through years of practice and self-denial.

Place a medium-sized rubber band over your index and middle finger. Close your hand into a fist. How quickly can you get the band onto the ring and little finger? A couple of seconds? Now try it this way...

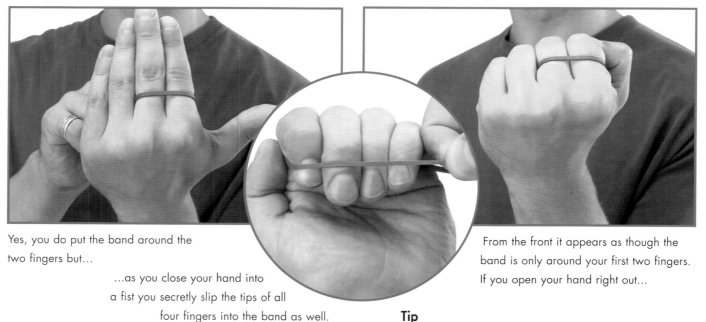

Yes, you do put the band around the two fingers but...

...as you close your hand into a fist you secretly slip the tips of all four fingers into the band as well.

From the front it appears as though the band is only around your first two fingers. If you open your hand right out...

Tip
• Practise getting all four fingertips into the band secretly, so that it appears to the audience as if you are just making the band more comfortable on only two fingers.

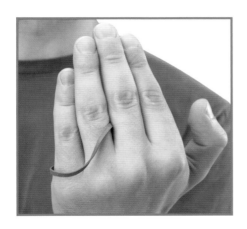

...and then back into a fist, you will find the band has jumped to the other two fingers automatically. Could it be easier?

It will also jump back again by exactly the same method.

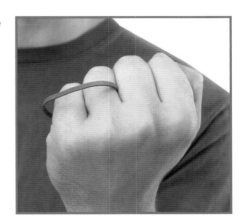

In fact you can work with two bands simultaneously and they will swap places.

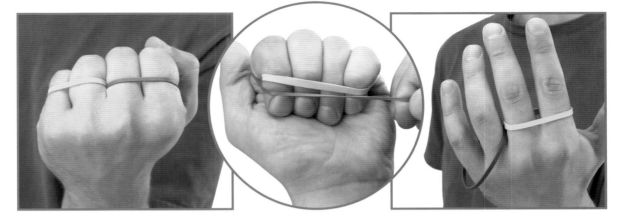

Performance notes

Try presenting this trick in three parts, each one apparently more challenging to you, and thus more amazing to the spectators, than the last.

1 A single band jumps as you click the fingers of the other hand.
2 You make two bands swap places as you wave a silk handkerchief over the hand.
3 You have locked the tips of your fingers together with a third band but still they swap in the time it takes for your hand to dive into a paper bag and come out again.

Clicking fingers, silk handkerchiefs and paper bags? Just dressing the trick up. It is called showmanship. Locking your fingers together with a third band? It does not make the trick any more difficult. Again, this is just showmanship, but it is still important, as your aim should be to entertain with a show not to just display a puzzle.

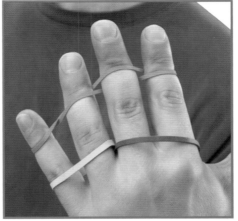

Tips

• I hope it is obvious that if you are making two bands swap places they must be of different colours, or your audience will not notice that anything has happened at all!
• This is an easy effect to learn, so put all of your effort into the presentation. Do not dismiss it because of its simplicity. This is actually a trick that I use as part of my management training seminars. It demonstrates that something doesn't have to be complicated to be effective. If they do not know the trick, you will certainly fool and entertain people with this one – and they do not have to be management consultants to enjoy it.

Note

• I have arranged some routines into a series of three a few times in this book. For some reason this always seems to greatly enhance the power of an effect on an audience. No one quite knows why, so maybe it's real magic.

Mathe... ...magical Mental Arithmetic

THE TITLE is a mouthful, but the magic arithmetic is surprisingly easy to do. If you can subtract 2 from a number and can also add up to 9, then you can do this. Try it on the blackboard at school and you will amaze your teachers and friends. They will not be able to do it as fast as you – even on a calculator!

The plot is that you invite someone to write any five-figure number on the board. Even while they are still writing you start to write a prediction in one corner of the board.

Then, in turn, you both write two more five-figure numbers into the main sum. Now get someone to add them all together with their calculator and incredibly the total will match your prediction.

Performance note

You can begin writing your prediction before the spectator starts to write his first number, as you know that yours will always begin with the figure **2**.

Any number is written down. For example: **57420**. To make your prediction, put a **2** in front of this number and subtract **2** from the final two digits. So it becomes: **257418**

Now as he writes his second number under the first, you simultaneously (well almost) write another above it.

69430 (yours)
57420
30569 (his)

For each digit that he writes, you write the number that would make his up to **9**. For instance, he writes a **7**, you write a **2** (because **7 + 2 = 9**).

Now do the same again. As soon as he has written a digit you can immediately write one.

81...
69430
57420
30569
184...

Tip

Once you have written your prediction, cover it with a piece of paper. You can then reveal it dramatically after the calculation has been completed.

Finally get someone to add all the figures together:

81526
+ 69430
+ 57420
+ 30569
+ 18473
= 257418

Performance note

Try asking other people to call out the numbers to be used. It is always fun to have some audience participation and then they will know that you are not using stooges.

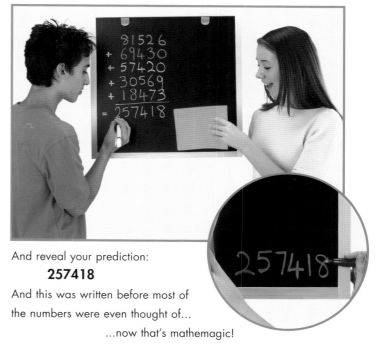

And reveal your prediction:

257418

And this was written before most of the numbers were even thought of...

...now that's mathemagic!

Tip

Once finished, it would be best to rub it off the board – otherwise, given time, your maths teacher might be able to work out some of the method.

Skip Snip

IT SOUNDS like something you would only expect from a school bully. You take a skipping rope and you cut it into two. However, you can do something that no bully can do. You can put it back together without knots, glue or a needle and thread. Of course, you use your magic... oh yes, and a little gimmick, or fake rope, hidden in your hand, but we don't tell anyone about that, do we?

So what is this gimmick? It is simply a small extra loop of rope that matches the skipping rope.

Tip

• Soft cotton rope is best and can be found in many DIY stores. If you cannot find matching rope, then either, if they are cheap, buy two skipping ropes and cut one up to make the gimmick or replace the rope in your skipping rope with one that is easily obtained.

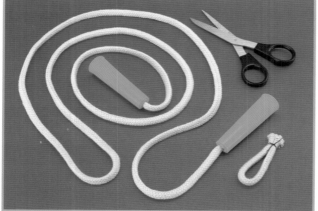

Notice how I have tied the gimmick into a loop with a little thread (see notes).

Notes

• Tying the gimmick into a loop makes it easier to handle and easier to make sure that you have it the right way round in your hand.

• Notice in the picture (left) how the loop is clipped between the scissor handles. Assuming you are right-handed, keep them like this in your left jacket pocket. You reach in to get the scissors and then pass them to your right hand. The gimmick is then very easy to leave in your left hand. It all happens in one natural movement, as all magic should.

• Of course, it does not have to be a skipping rope. Think laterally. Think washing line, think shoelace, even think wire and wire cutters. Make it suit you.

Pass out the scissors to a volunteer. This is when you secure the gimmick in your hand. Take back the rope by its middle and place it into your left fist so that the centre loop is exposed.

What you don't expose is that as you put the centre of the rope into your fist, you leave it hidden by your fingers and actually pull the top of the gimmick into view.

Pass out the skipping rope for inspection. Someone in your audience could even try it out, but not near a shelf full of ornaments! Casually show that both your hands are empty.

The volunteer cuts the rope. No one could argue that the rope is not now well and truly cut.

You take back the scissors and trim off the messy ends. In reality you trim away all of the gimmick letting it fall in small pieces to the floor

You are now all set to do your magic. It would also look good for the audience if a volunteer on each side of you slowly pulled the rope taut. Then you take a bow and thank your helpers.

Close-Up Magic

Naked Thumb

I SUPPOSE FOR a trick to be truly impromptu you should be able to perform it anywhere, at any time. You have just stepped out of the shower and your four-year-old son says, 'Show us a trick, Dad' as he drags his nursery school teacher into the room. So you need a trick requiring absolutely no props at all.

First...
Show your thumb.

Take hold of it with your other hand.

Pull the thumb into two parts.

The secret – as you go to grab your thumb, you actually bend it inwards and place the tip of your other thumb in its place. The photo (below left) shows the move exposed. Practise this until you can do it very quickly in one smooth action. The changeover will not then be noticed.

Tips
• All these thumb moves should be done quite rapidly, and in quick succession, to make the illusion perfect. If you give someone time to stop and stare at your hands in the 'trick' position, they might easily work out the method.

• Practise this one in front of a mirror. It looks really weird. You may fool yourself! If you do, remember not to faint.

Now...

Show your thumb in this new position.

Grab it again and stretch it to about three times its normal length.

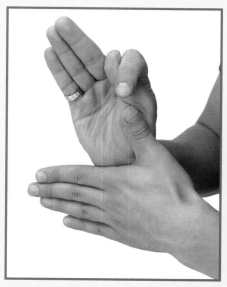

Once again, hidden by the grabbing movement, the thumbs swap places. Look at the 'behind the scenes' shot of the previous photo and you will see how.

And finally...

This time you are going to grab the whole thumb. Hold it tight in your fist.

Pull it right away. Done quickly this is a great illusion.

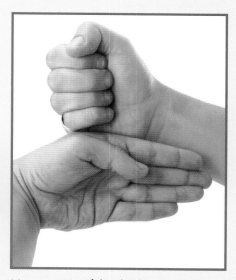

No swapping of thumbs this time, you simply tuck your thumb right down into your palm as soon as the 'grabbing' hand comes over and hides it from the spectator's view.

Note
- Oh, by the way, his nursery school teacher is also his mother!

Rise and Fall

As YOU opened the book at this page, you will have noticed the free gift of 10 metres of invisible thread. If it is not there, it may have fallen into your lap or even to the floor. Can you see it? I hope not, it's supposed to be invisible.

OK, stop searching now, I'm joking but you will certainly be able to obtain thread or line that is so thin that it is almost invisible. In fact in front of the right background and taking care with your 'angles' your audience will simply not be able to see it. Apart from magic shops, sources include haberdashers for ultra fine thread, fishing shops for the thinnest fishing line, or even a long human hair. Ask before you take one of the latter or you may get a bonus slap in the face for free.

Before we get into the thread tricks, try this quick gag. When questioned about using invisible thread, pretend to admit it.

Take an imaginary piece out of your pocket and hold it between your hands. Move your hands about but keep them the same distance apart as if connected by a thread.

Ask your challenger to take hold of one end and to hold his other hand on the mid-point to see if he can 'feel it'.

Ask him to pull hard on his end on the count of three. One, two, three...

Call out 'Not that hard!' as you slap your hand against his. (Make sure that you don't really hurt him, just give him a surprise.)

He won't challenge you about invisible threads again!

Ring up

A borrowed ring begins to levitate when it is put on a penciL.

Do the preparation first. A fine thread is attached to your clothes or belt at around waist level. The free end has a small blob of sticky tac attached to it and this in turn is stuck onto a trouser stud or jacket button. (The thread has been made obvious here for the photograph.)

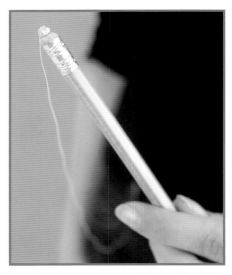

Ask someone to examine the pencil and then borrow a ring. While they remove their ring you secretly attach the thread to the top of the pencil.

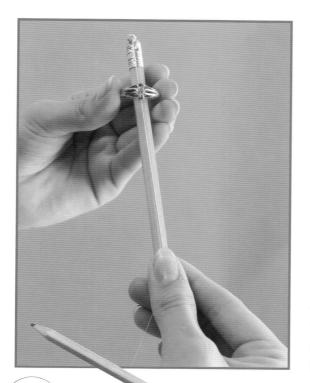

Keeping the thread hidden behind the pencil with your thumb, drop the ring over the pencil.

Very gently, let the ring rest on the thread and your hand and take up any slack in the thread by moving the pencil away from your body. This movement should be imperceptible.

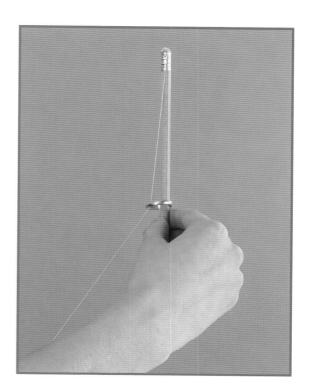

Tips

• If you are performing this as part of a show, use your magic wand instead of a pencil.

• The fixed end of the thread can be attached to a safety pin for easy set-up and the free end attached anywhere that it is not obvious to a spectator and yet where you can easily and secretly pick it up in your fingers.

• For quicker attachment, customize your pencil by removing the rubber eraser and filling the hole with sticky tac. It will look just like the rubber. A knot at the end of your thread stops it pulling out of the sticky tac too easily.

• The best thread length can only be determined by trial and error during your practice sessions.

Misdirect by using your other hand to introduce 'magic forces', while you make the ring rise by slowly moving the pencil away from you.

As you remove the ring in order to return it (yes, you do have to return the ring!), pull the thread away from the tac and let it hang down unnoticed until you can remove it without being seen.

Light ink

This is a variation of the 'Ring Up' trick and it may well suit some people better. It does not involve borrowing anything although there is no reason why the pen cannot be borrowed if it is of the right type.

The set-up is much the same except that you will need only a very tiny blob of sticky tac on the free end of the thread.

Take apart your pen and hand the centre out, asking someone if they think the ink is light or dark. They will probably take a careful look, holding it up to the light. Use this moment to get hold of the free end of your thread.

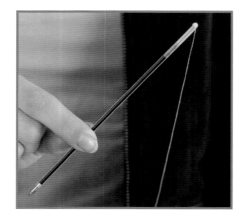

'The answer is BOTH', you say, 'dark but also very light.' You take back the refill and hand out the main body and cap.

As they look at these, stick the blob of tac onto the end of the refill.

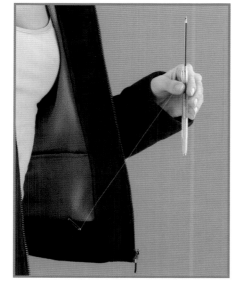

Offer to demonstrate as you take back the pen body and insert the refill into it upside down. Although the thread is very fine, screen it with your arm during these actions, just in case.

Take back the cap and hold it above the pen and start to make the refill rise by imperceptibly moving the pen away from you. It certainly is 'light' – it's floating!

Tips

• Consider carefully the clothes that you are wearing when doing magic with threads.
• A black thread will be too obvious in front of a white shirt and nylon line can often be seen glinting in the light in front of black clothing.
• Always check first in front of a mirror.
• Clothing with a pattern is often best, as the thread cannot be made out against the busy background.

Act as if the cap was an important part of the effect. The audience might even think that you have a magnet hidden in it.

After the refill has gone back down hand them the cap again. While they are looking even more closely at it, take out the refill and remove the thread from it during the action of handing both parts over for inspection.

Allow the thread to drop unnoticed to your side as before.

Torn and Restored Tissue

THIS IS certainly a classic of magic. For centuries magicians have been destroying things in front of an audience and then restoring them to their original state. Tearing up a tissue is a good first routine in this genre.

You have probably already guessed that in order to prepare you will need two identical pieces of tissue paper.

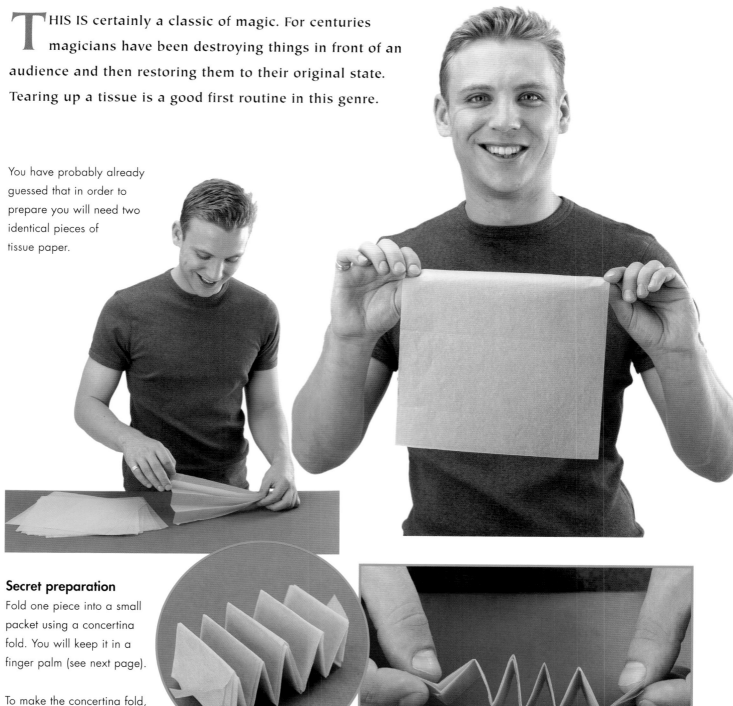

Secret preparation

Fold one piece into a small packet using a concertina fold. You will keep it in a finger palm (see next page).

To make the concertina fold, first zig-zag fold the tissue as shown in the picture above. Then zig-zag along its length as shown right. The two outer corners (inset) are curled outwards so that you can find them easily for the restoration.

Show the audience the sheet that you are going to tear. The fake is secured in your left hand – but it looks empty, doesn't it?

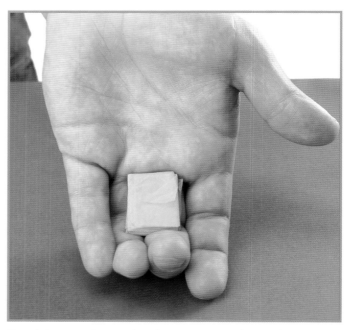

The ability to make your hand appear empty shows what a good sleight finger-palming is.

Finger-palming tip

- Finger-palm a coin or a piece of tissue and then look in a mirror to check just how much you can open and tilt your hand in various directions without it being seen. Magicians call this 'checking their angles'. You will be amazed at what you can get away with.

Tear the tissue into smaller and smaller pieces…

...bringing the fake into position behind the bits as you go…

Bring the pieces up to your mouth to give them a magic blow. OK, the blow does nothing but this position allows the audience to see that your hands are otherwise empty and...

...as you lower your hands again you turn the pieces to move the fake to the front and slowly and magically start to unfold it.

The pieces now appear to be fully restored.

Keep the torn pieces in a bundle behind your fingertips and take your bow.

Tip
• As soon as you have taken your bow, crumple up the restored piece with the torn 'evidence' and throw it all out of sight into your magic box.

• Make your presentation a bit more wacky and off the wall – how about torn and restored toilet paper! The central tube would make the perfect place to conceal the folded piece for the restoration. Perhaps this is not to everyone's taste but it is lateral thinking like this that helps make your magic original and memorable.

A Short Break

HOPEFULLY audiences will always appreciate your magical skills, but they usually like it even more if you appear to let them make the magic happen themselves. In this effect the spectator initially breaks your favourite magic match but you lend him some magic power so that he can make it as good as new.

Show a match and claim that it is a very special match that you have had for years and years and that you have made it unbreakable.

Holding it between your fingers as shown, move your hands as if you were bending the match up and down. In fact only your hands move. The match stays still within your fingers and does not bend. To a spectator, however, it does appear to flex.

Let a spectator try to break your unbreakable match, but, so that he does not risk getting splinters, cover the match with a handkerchief.

Unfortunately, when he tries to bend it, he does break the match. You look very upset about the loss of your pet match (!) and demand that he does some magic to repair it.

Safety warning
Children should only use matches under adult supervision.

Ask him to blow gently on the broken match in the handkerchief. Then with an outstretched hand, take a corner of the handkerchief and gently shake it out.

The match will fall into his waiting hands fully restored.

So how do you do it?

Before you even begin, hide a match in the hem of your handkerchief.

As you apparently put the match up underneath the handkerchief, you do a switch. Bring up the gimmick match into your spectator's fingers and leave the original match in the fold of cloth that this will create.

When you gently shake out the handkerchief, the original match falls into his hands and the broken fake stays hidden in the hem.

Tips
• Place the gimmicked handkerchief into your pocket in such a way that you can easily find the fake and thus bring it out holding this corner.
• Shake out the handkerchief at the beginning and end of the trick to 'prove' that it is empty.

Smooth Get Away

This could be done as part of a magic act but just as easily as spur-of-the-moment magic in a restaurant or bar. You only need to find a couple of table napkins (preferably of contrasting colours), a straight-sided glass and a rubber band. In a magic act you would probably use brightly coloured silk handkerchiefs instead of the napkins. So, what is the trick?

The effect

A silk is put into a glass. Another silk is put over the top of the glass and tightly secured with an elastic band. Yet you – O Wondrous Magician – reach beneath the cover, penetrate the solid glass with your enchanted fingers and remove the trapped silk for all to see. Clever, eh?

Tips

• The silk in the glass must be large enough to ensure that it will not fall out as the glass is turned upside down.

• The cover silk must be opaque enough so that the audience cannot see through it during the inversion or later to discern which way up the glass is held.

• Be careful not to knock the silk or let any movement be seen as you invert the glass. Likewise as you turn it back again while removing the cover silk.

Performance notes

You will see how this effect could be performed impromptu in a bar. You might have to look around to find a rubber band but, hey, you're a magician so you always keep such useful things in your pocket or handbag – well, don't you?

Carefully push the first silk into the glass.

Cover the glass with the second silk.

Drag the silk over the top of the glass to ensure that your audience can clearly see the shape of the glass.

Secure the second silk with the rubber band.

Remove the imprisoned silk and then show the empty glass to your audience.

This is what the audience does not see. I am sure that this final picture has revealed the secret to you. As you bring the larger silk up in front of the glass in order to cover it, you make the 'move'. As soon as the glass is hidden behind the silk you simply invert it. The rest is all up to your acting skills. Don't forget to invert it again as you remove the cover or your cover will be well and truly blown!

Mouse Mat Gamble

NOT REALLY a gamble. Well, you are a magician, after all, so you are bound to win. Probably something to do with cheating, but let's keep that between you and me. Actually in this trick everyone wins – you just win more!

Tell two of your friends that you are taken by a sudden wave of extreme generosity. You have decided that you all deserve a bonus wage and so have placed three wage envelopes on your mouse mat. You move them all around until they tell you to stop, then each of your friends takes it in turn to choose one. You are left with the third and now they can open theirs. All three of you find a 1p coin.

'Did you not find anything else in yours?' you ask. 'Pity that you didn't choose this one then!' You say, as you pull a £5 note out of your envelope.

You will need three small wage envelopes with a 1p coin in each, a £5 note and a mouse mat.

The secret of your 'lucky' win? A folded £5 note is hidden under the edge of the mat. It just shows in the photo but, obviously, it shouldn't show when you do the trick.

Always pick up the envelopes in the same way. Fingers on top, thumb underneath.

Tips

• After the first choice, mix the envelopes around again, so that one is over the note. If they choose that one, move the next one into position as you say 'Are you sure that you don't want this one?' If they say no leave it in position. If they say yes, then give them that one and put the other back in 'position'. Could it seem fairer?

• Remember exactly where the £5 note is concealed by the pattern on the mat or by using a secret mark.

• Putting the 1p coin in the envelopes psychologically gives the spectators each a prize and stops them hating you too much for winning the fiver! Use any currency to suit.

When you get to pick up the last one, your thumb secretly pulls the note out behind the envelope. This happens just as the others start to open their 'prizes'. This gives you some misdirection.

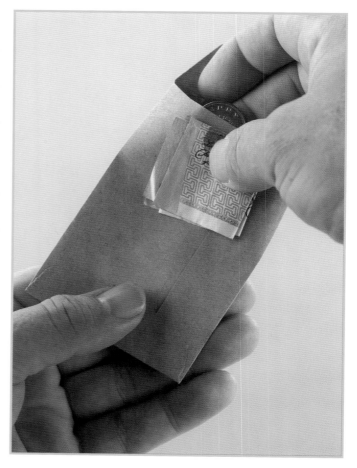

Simply pull the note up from behind the opened envelope. From their point of view it will look as if it comes from inside.

Ex-straw-dinary Magic

AS THE title suggests, this is some fun magic that you can do with drinking straws and so is perfect to perform in a restaurant or burger bar. The first effect is impromptu while the second requires just a little preparation.

Performance notes

• Hold the straws directly in front of your body and perform the moves slowly and deliberately.

• Afterwards, hand out some straws for others to have a go.

Straw knot...not!

This is one of those effects with which you will probably fool yourself as you seem to have securely twisted the two straws together and yet they apparently just melt apart. When your friends try to duplicate the trick, they will almost certainly tie themselves up in a knot.

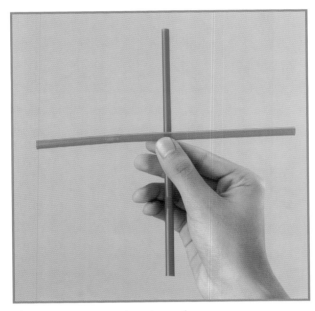

Place one straw over the other to form a cross

The left 'arm' is bent right around behind the vertical straw and then back to its first position.

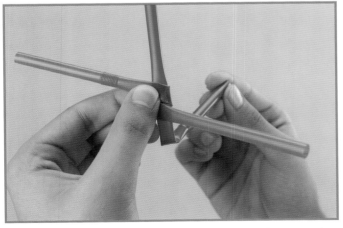

Now the lower 'leg' is bent up behind the right-hand 'arm' and back over it to its previous position.

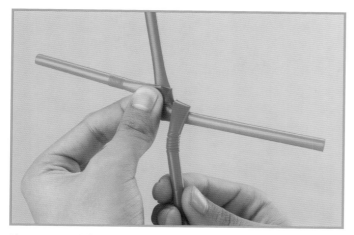

The straws will form a cross again but will be firmly twisted together at the centre, as shown.

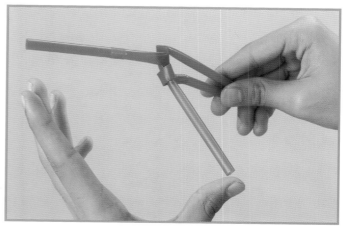

Now take hold of the vertical straw from the back and the horizontal straw from the front.

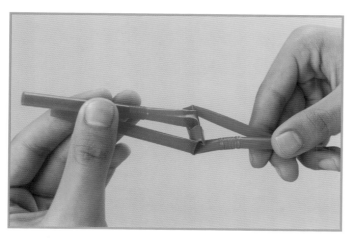

As you begin to pull apart the straws will 'catch' together and still appear to be inextricably joined.

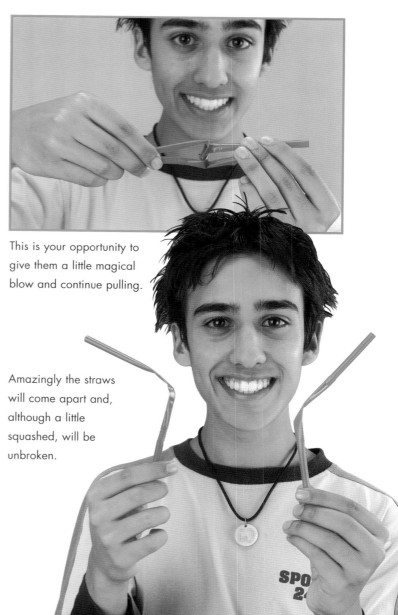

This is your opportunity to give them a little magical blow and continue pulling.

Amazingly the straws will come apart and, although a little squashed, will be unbroken.

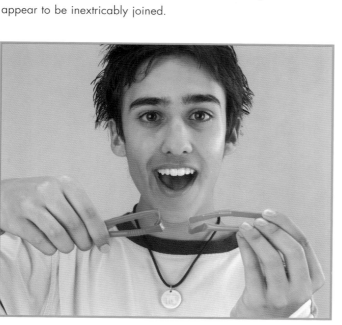

An Ex-straw-dinary Cut

The only preparation that is required in this effect is to make a longitudinal slit in the straw measuring about 4cm (1½ in) near its centre. This obviously needs to be done out of sight of your friends so either keep a straw from an earlier visit to the restaurant and prepare it at home or nip into the bathroom and prepare one there. The slit is very easily made, as straws are not built to become long-lasting family heirlooms. A blade, table knife, pin or sometimes even a fingernail will suffice. Just casually leave the straw on the table amongst everything else and pick it up when you are ready to do the trick. It must not seem to be a special straw.

If someone tries to use it in the meantime and they get drink all over themselves, then forget the trick in case they conjure you up a dry-cleaning bill!

The straw has been prepared with a slit as shown here.

Warning
• Always take care when using knives and other sharp objects.

Borrow something like a shoelace, cord from a neck pendant or safety string from a pair of glasses (but also have a length of string in your pocket just in case you can't find anything suitable).

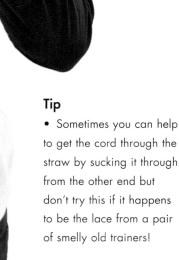

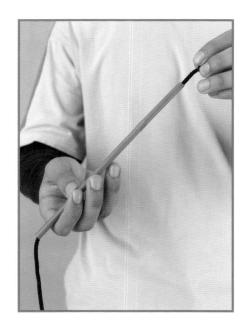

Tip
• Sometimes you can help to get the cord through the straw by sucking it through from the other end but don't try this if it happens to be the lace from a pair of smelly old trainers!

Now bend the straw in half making sure that the slit is on the inside of the bend.

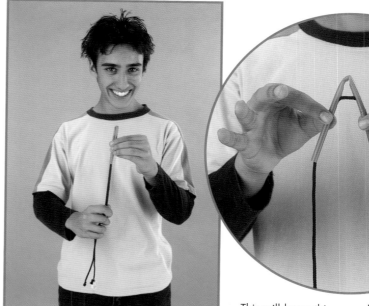

Ask someone to pass you a tableknife or a pair of scissors, secretly pulling down on the ends of the cord as you do so.

This will leave things as shown but, when the straw is folded, the audience will not be able to see the cord.

Cut right through the straw at the bend but above the cord. Let every one see the straw is cleanly cut but do not allow them to look down into the straw(s). Surely you must have cut the cord in half.

Immediately hold the straw straight, back in line again, and pull out the cord, now magically restored – or should that be restrawed? Crumple up the halves of the straw and throw them away in order to remove any 'evidence' from the scene.

The Strangest String

THIS IS how to make up a special piece of string that will apparently pass through almost anything. You can thread the string through all kinds of solid loops, such as the handle of a mug, a metal coat hanger, or the arm of a wooden chair, and yet it always escapes. Here it is going to pass through the arm of your volunteer.

Prepare the string. It has two beads threaded onto it and a large knot tied at each end.

Hold both beads in one hand and then...

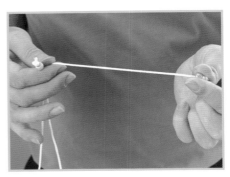

...take one bead in the other hand and pull as shown until the string is taut. This is the 'fair' display of the string and can be repeated as you introduce the trick.

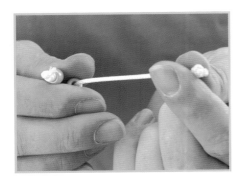

When you are ready to perform the trick you appear to do the same again but actually you leave both beads hidden in your fingers and only take hold of the knot.

You are now ready but no one realizes that you have done anything yet.

A friend locks his arms into a loop and you thread the string through. Surely there can be no escape?

As you show that the string does go right around their arm, bring your hands together and secretly get hold of a bead in each hand.

Quickly pull your hands, and the beads, apart.

Faster than the eye can see, the free end of the string will fly around their arm and...

...you will be left holding a taut string that is no longer threaded around their arm. It MUST have gone clean through their flesh. Well, if we believe that, then the audience will as well.

Important note: If your friend's arm falls off, then you need more practice!

Tip
• To make the gimmick, use fine strong nylon cord and beads of a size that you can hide behind your fingers. Glass beads are good, as they will slide easily along the cord.

Photo Card

IF YOU have a computer with a photo-workshop programme, then have a go at this trick. If you do not have access to such technology, then you can just as effectively make up the trick with pieces of card and draw cartoon 'stick men' onto them.

Ask someone to take a photograph of you holding a playing card. Then either take another without the card or digitally remove the card using your computer software.

Print the cards out on a sheet with some blank space beneath each picture and cut them up into a handy size. If you intend to do the trick several times, you will need at least six without the playing card and sufficient with the card to allow you to use one each time you perform the effect.

Tip
• Playing cards could also be digitally added to existing photos – the graphics can be found in many computer folders of clip art. You could also vary the playing card so that you are not always having to force the same one. This is important if you perform the trick to several people who know each other. They are hardly likely to think it a coincidence that they all happened to choose the same card. They might think that you are cheating. Perish the thought!

Cut one of the 'without card' cards approximately in half and discard the lower blank part. This goes on top of your stack of identical cards but with one of the special 'with card' photos directly below it.

Secure a wide rubber band around the whole stack hiding the cut edge. It will appear to be a packet of identical 'without card' cards. A sliver of double-sided tape under the band helps to keep the top half-card from falling out.

Show the stack of cards to your spectator and explain that you have made them in anticipation of becoming a world-famous magician. You will then be able to hand out autographs on them. You can actually pull out, and then return, one of the backmost cards as you speak.

Admit to not being very famous yet so ask for the spectator's autograph on the top card instead of yours. Make sure that they sign in the white space.

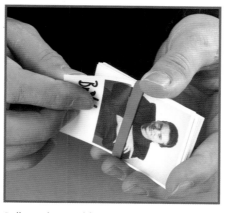

Pull out the card by its lower end and put it face down on the table or part way into your pocket.

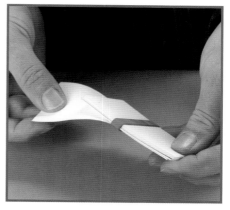

As you pull the card out briefly turn the whole pack face down by rolling your wrist. This way no one will see that the top card is only a half card. This move is called a 'wrist kill'.

Now state that you will prove your worth as a magician by attempting a card trick. Force the card, in this case the ace of clubs, on the spectator (see 'card forcing' pages 95-97). Now, using your best acting skills, fail to find the card.

Say that you suppose that the spectator will not want your photograph now and hand it to her to dispose of as she wishes.

When she looks at it she will see that incredibly the picture has now changed into one of you holding her chosen card!

Notes

• I didn't realize, until I made the cards for this trick, just how good it would be. I think I may well begin to regularly use this trick in my own professional repertoire, so please do not tell anyone how to do it!

• The idea of the half card on the stack is a very old one and is known by magicians as the 'out to lunch' principle.

Tips

• A bit of finesse here would be to control the chosen card to the top, as you search for it. While the spectator is looking at the photograph, take this opportunity to palm off the top card and hide it in your pocket (see 'palming' page 98). Now you can say that the reason that you could not find the card was that it had vanished into the photo. If the spectator looks through the pack she will not find the ace of clubs.

• You can also flick through the stack of photo-cards to show that no others have a playing card on them.

Ringback

IN THIS EFFECT you borrow a lady's ring, but tell her not to worry as you wrap it in a handkerchief and give it to a responsible member of your audience to hold. Next, produce or borrow a pencil, which can be held by a single spectator, or even two spectators, one at each end. Wouldn't it be great if you could make the ring vanish from the handkerchief and end up threaded onto the pencil even though the helper never lets go of the ends?

Here's how...

The ring and the pencil are just as they seem to be, but the handkerchief is decidedly dodgy!

When you put the real ring under the handkerchief, push the fake ring up to the top and keep the real ring in a finger palm in your hand.

Construction

The handkerchief has a curtain ring sewn into the hem at one corner.

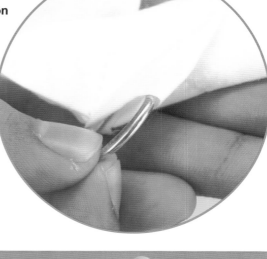

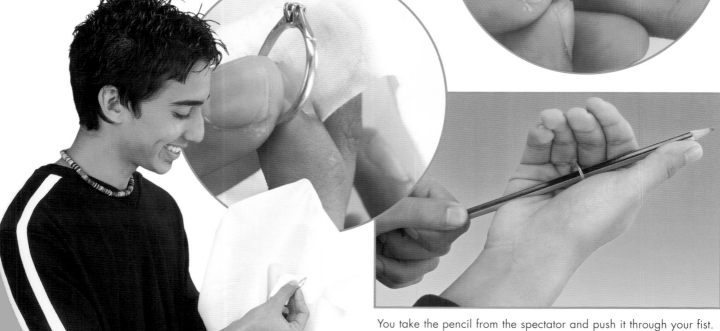

You take the pencil from the spectator and push it through your fist. Secretly you make sure that it slides through the ring.

A spectator holds each end of the pencil.

You take the handkerchief and fake ring from the person holding it and drape it over your hand.

Make a little magic 'wave' over the handkerchief. Take time here as it should look like you are trying to make the magic work.

First remove your hand and then whisk the handkerchief away.

This should leave the ring spinning on the pencil. Solid has passed through solid.

Take a bow and enjoy your applause!

Tips

• Instead of the pencil you could use your magic wand. Always try to be original if you can. Why not use the 'mint-with-the-hole' and a knitting needle? Or – one for the workshop – a metal washer onto six-inch nail. Be creative and make the trick your own.

• Do not give the ring in the handkerchief to the ring's owner to hold, as he or she might be able to recognize that it is a different ring by feel. Try to borrow a ring that is about the same thickness as the fake ring.

Fission Impossible

IS IT POSSIBLE to tie a knot in a rope without letting go of the ends? In theory, knot (sorry!) – well, not unless the rope was miraculously to separate. Hence the fission. Here are two methods. The first will require a little practice. The second is really a joke solution to the problem, but at least it requires no practice whatsoever (hurray!).

Magic Version

This really is worth learning, as it will drive your friends mad that they cannot do it and they can't see how you do it, however closely they look.

Follow the moves with a piece of rope in your hands and don't worry about the left-hand end. All the action happens with the right.

Hold the rope in both hands as shown, right.

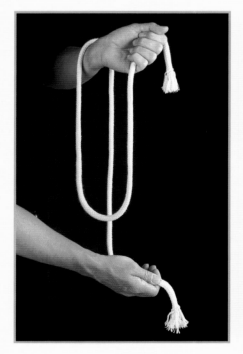

The right-hand end goes over the left wrist...

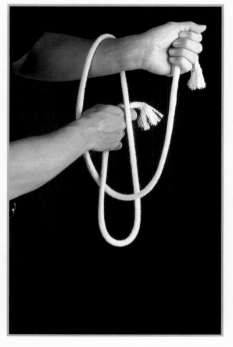

...into the loop...around the front of the forward part...

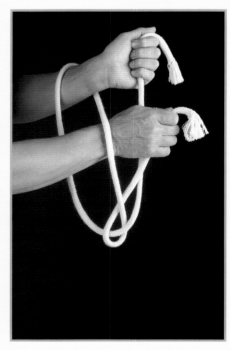

...and back out again. You should now have something that looks like this.

The next stage should look as though you simply tip your hands forward, to let the ropes slide off, while not letting go of the ends.

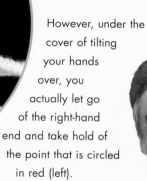

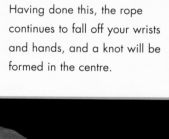

However, under the cover of tilting your hands over, you actually let go of the right-hand end and take hold of the point that is circled in red (left).

Tip

• Once again, just practise until you can do the whole routine with a smooth action and a steady rhythm, hardly needing to look at your hands.

Having done this, the rope continues to fall off your wrists and hands, and a knot will be formed in the centre.

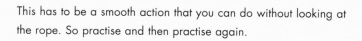

This has to be a smooth action that you can do without looking at the rope. So practise and then practise again.

Fission Impossible – Easy Version

Put the rope on the table and simply cross your arms.

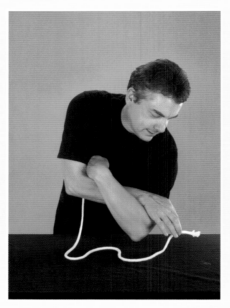

Take hold of one end of the rope in each hand.

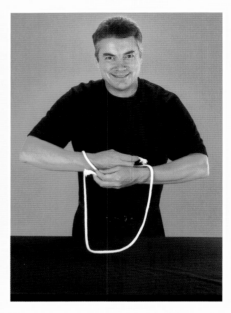

Uncross your arms.

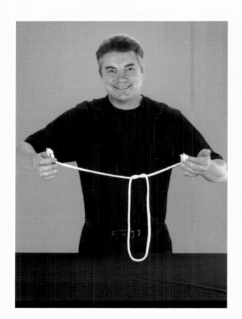

Could it be simpler?

Link Up

THIS IS a classic impromptu magic effect that is perfect for the office or workplace as it uses a rubber band and paperclips. It also requires a piece of paper. A bank note is ideal as it is strong and resists tearing. This trick has been around for many, many years and for a very good reason. It's weird and completely baffling. Because it takes place so quickly, even you won't be able to see quite how it happens.

First, fold the note in half lengthways and hang a rubber band on its mid-point...

...then zigzag fold the note as shown...

...then on either side of the rubber band, clip the outer section of the note to the mid section, as shown. Do not clip all three sections in the one clip.

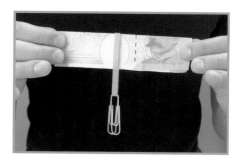

Pull quite sharply on the ends of the note. Not only will both paperclips have found their way onto the rubber band but also...

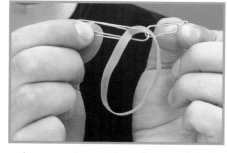

...the paperclips will have become linked to each other!

All three items are now linked together and you were not even touching them. Weird! It will probably take you longer to undo them all again than it took you to do the trick in the first place.

Mobile Money Mystery

THIS ONE requires a little preparation and some 'bottle' or nerve. What it gives back is a stunner of an effect with a 'kicker' finish that will blow people's socks off.

You borrow a £5 note from a friend (that might be your first miracle!). You key the note's number into your mobile phone and text it to a friend on the other side of the room. You fold the note into a piece of paper or tissue and give it to another trusted friend to hold for a while.

Now ask for the text to be forwarded back to your phone. As soon as your phone beeps to say that the text has arrived, hand it to someone to read the message. They won't be able to because the screen is blank and the phone appears to be off. Then, when the piece of paper is unfolded the note has vanished. Now ask the person holding your phone to switch it on. They won't be able to as there is no battery or SIM card in the phone!

Now for the finale. When they open the phone they find a folded £5 note in place of the battery, and the number matches the one recorded in the other mobile phone.

Breaking the routine down, there are basically two parts.

Part 1. Sending and receiving a text with a 'dead' mobile phone

First, the preparation. Next time you upgrade your phone, keep your old one for this type of trick. Load it with a folded £5 note, having first noted its number.

The number is already keyed into your real phone as a text message, along with your friend's mobile number. All you have to do is press the send button. This is prepared to stand out from the rest with an old shirt button and some sticky tack.

The real phone could be hidden up your sleeve secured by a rubber band or even in your breast pocket. Anywhere that you can surreptitiously press the send button when required. This should be easy, as it sticks out far enough!

Meanwhile, sending the text with the dead phone is all acting. Just press some buttons and don't let anyone see the screen. Pretend that you are reading the serial number from the note.

Part 2. The vanish of the note

First, the preparation. Place an empty folded piece of paper in your pocket along with a note pad or piece of paper.

Fold the note up small and, as you remove the pad from your pocket, get the empty packet into a finger palm.

Wrap the note in the paper and ask if you can leave it in a trusted friend's jacket pocket for safekeeping.

As you walk over to drop it into their pocket, use your thumb to pull back the packet with the note and push forward the empty one. This 'switch' is covered by the larger movements of you walking and moving your arm.

Now, as you ask for the text to be returned, stand impatiently with your hands in your pockets and stare at the phone on the table. This gives you the opportunity to 'ditch' the full packet in your pocket.

A jacket pocket is a good place to leave the 'empty' packet, as your helper is less likely to fiddle with it and discover that it is empty, too early. Also just hope that your Mum doesn't phone you in the middle of your trick!

Don't forget to give the £5 note back to its original owner at the end!

Note

When receiving the text don't worry about the sound coming from the wrong place. No one can ever hear exactly where it's coming from; haven't you noticed when someone receives a text on the train, everyone nearby reaches for their pockets?

The Rate of Knots

ROPE TRICKS are always popular in close-up magic, as you can hand the rope out for inspection and your audience can give it a good old tug. Now it's not the 'good old tug' that is going to travel at a rate of knots but your fingers as you declare that you are going to tie a knot faster than anyone else in the world.

To make this into a routine I have divided the magic into three stages: a corny old gag followed by two tricks.

Stage 1: The gag

Dangle the rope from your hand. 'Do you want to see the world's fastest knot?'

Flick the rope. 'Do you want to see it again? I actually tied it and untied it in less than a millionth of a second.'

OK, it is an old gag but it sets you up nicely for stage 3, later on.

Stage 2: Speed knot

Lay the rope over your hands as shown. Note that it hangs freely over the back of one hand and the front of the other.

Now bring your hands together and clip the loose ends between the first and second fingers of the opposite hand. Keeping hold of the ends, pull your hands apart and a knot will be formed in the middle.

Practise this until you can do it really, really quickly.

After stage 2, relax as if your routine has finished and begin to untie the knot.

Stage 3: Instant knot

However, what you actually do is to move the knot close to one end and keep it hidden in your hand.

When you are ready, announce that you will try the first trick again as no one seemed to believe you.

Flick the rope out – nothing happens.

Continue to flick the rope out two or three times – nothing happens.

Just when the audience are starting to think that you are playing another joke on them, keep hold of the wrong end and flick out the knotted end.

It will still look like the same action but suddenly the audience will realize that now there really is a knot in the rope.

You have done the impossible knot!

Tips
• The relaxing between stages 2 and 3 is an integral part of the routine because if you look relaxed and take a step back, as if the routine was over, then the audience will relax as well. This way the 'heat' will be off you while you prepare stage 3. It is a form of misdirection.
• Use soft cotton cord. It is available in many DIY and outdoor pursuits stores, as well as from magic dealers.

Two in the Hand – One in the Pocket

THIS IS A classic series of moves that can be done with all sorts of small objects. Here we use peanuts, as they are something you can often find at a party, pub or restaurant. You apparently do the trick with three but in fact you will need four. You will also need a surprise 'load' for your big finish to the trick. How about a peanut still in its shell or a walnut, or even a wing-nut or locknut from the workshop?

Before you even begin the trick hide a peanut between the fingers of your right hand and make sure that you have something to use for your finish in your right-hand jacket pocket. Here, I use a walnut.

Call for three peanuts. Ask a spectator to show them in their hand or on the table.

Pick up one peanut and put it in your left hand.
'One in the hand.'

Pick up another and also put it in your left hand but secretly add the one hidden in your right hand.
'Two in the hand.'

Tips

• Pace and timing are very important here. As you practise this trick, try to acquire a steady rhythm so that each move has an equal beat.

• Find objects to do the trick with that suit your personality, your hands, your pockets and your sense of humour.

Pick up the last peanut and apparently put it in your pocket. Actually hide it between your fingers as before.

'And one in the pocket.'

'How many in my hand?'
Most people will say two,
but you show three.

Repeat the whole process one more time but when you have shown the three in your hand this time, instead of bringing the peanut out of your pocket, you bring out the walnut hidden in your hand.

Now pick up two of the peanuts and pretend to put them into your left hand but you actually put the walnut there.
'Two in the hand.'

Pick up the last peanut and put it into your pocket (along with the other two).
'One in the pocket.'
'How many in my hand?'

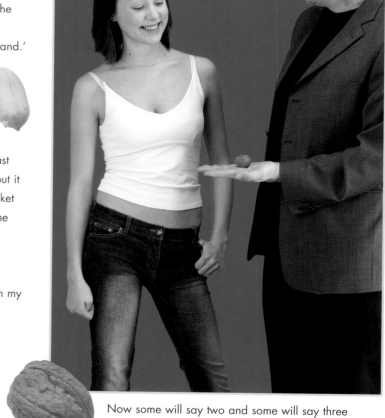

Now some will say two and some will say three but no one will expect the walnut!

Tea Party

IT IS a commonly held belief that a tea party is where people go to socialize over a cup of tea. In fact, it is the tea that likes to socialize and will use any excuse to get together for a party. Now, some might think that I am actually using a feeble quip to construct a patter line for this trick. I will let you, patient reader, decide.

The effect

You show four teabags and four teacups. If possible, use one cup that is fancier than the rest; you can call this one the party cup. The story goes that all the teabags want to be in the party cup, so magically transport themselves there one by one.

For this trick you will have to learn one sleight of hand move. It is basically a 'fingerclip false pass'. Once learned, you will find this a very useful sleight that you can use with many small objects, including coins. Basically it should look as if you are passing something, in this instance a teabag, from one hand to the other but in fact you retain it in the first hand.

Historical fact

• Tricks involving hiding objects under cups and making them transfer to another cup, disappear or transform into other objects are some of the oldest recorded. Magicians have been performing similar tricks for thousands of years.

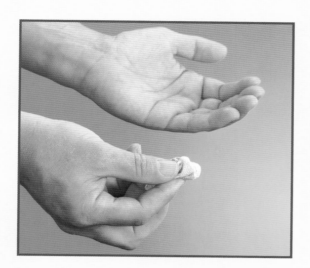

The false pass

You hold the bag between thumb and forefinger as shown but you are also clipping part of it between your second and third fingertips.

As you place the bag into the palm of your left hand three things happen simultaneously:

1 Your left fingers begin to close over the bag.
2 Your right thumb and forefinger let the bag go.
3 The second and third fingers of your right hand curl inwards taking the bag with them.

Now your right thumb and forefinger can clearly be seen to be empty where a moment before they held the bag. Your left fist is closed apparently holding the teabag. The actual bag is hidden in your right fist – you can just see it from this angle but the spectator, who is in front of you, cannot.

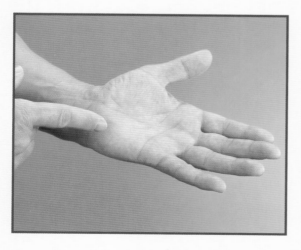

Tip

• Let your eyes follow the movement of the hand that is meant to be holding the bag. Do not look at your right hand.

• When practising, sometimes pass the bag normally and sometimes do the false pass. There should be no discernible difference. Practise it in front of a mirror to test this.

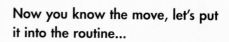

Now you know the move, let's put it into the routine...

Stage one

Show the four cups and four teabags in a line, ensuring the audience can clearly see that all the cups are empty.

Pick up the teabag in your right hand and pass it to your left – then pick up the cup in your right hand, as shown.

Drop the teabag into the cup and invert the cup onto the table quite quickly so that the teabag doesn't fall out.
Repeat the same for the second cup.

But when you get to the third cup, pick up the teabag as before but do the false pass.

Drop 'nothing' into the cup.

Invert the empty cup in the same way as before.

For the fourth cup, pick up the last teabag and pass it into your other hand along with the concealed one. It should appear to be one bag only.

Drop two teabags, as if they were one, into the cup.

Invert the cup as before. There will now be one bag under each of the first two cups, nothing under the third cup and two bags under the fourth. The audience will believe there is a bag under each cup.

Stage two

Turn over the first cup with your left hand. Pick up the teabag with your right hand and do a false pass into your left hand. Open your left hand to show that the teabag has 'vanished'.

Immediately pick up the fourth cup to show two teabags.

The first magic transposition has happened! Count the two teabags back into the fourth cup, secretly adding the concealed teabag.

Do the same for the teabag that is under the second cup.

Guess what?

You do not have to do any clever stuff to vanish the teabag under the third cup, as there is nothing there.

The audience just thinks that there is.

So this time, simply click your fingers over the third cup.

This will really confuse them because when you lift the cup, the teabag has vanished!

Finally, lift the last cup and there are all four teabags having their party. Well, OK, just lying in a heap then.

So take your well-deserved applause and make yourself a nice cup of tea.

Tip

• This trick will take some practice to get it to flow smoothly but the end result will be well worth it. You will have mastered a brilliant false pass that you can use time and time again in your magic performances.

Anti-magnetic Matches

MY FATHER is not a magician but when I was a young boy he completely and utterly fooled me with this one. In fact, it was probably the first close-up magic trick I ever saw. He took two matches, laid one on his hand and rubbed the other gently on his sleeve. Then he brought the heads of the two matches close together and the one on his hand flew into the air. I couldn't believe my eyes and went away rubbing matches on my sleeve.

Yes, they were safety matches – I wasn't that silly.

Eventually, after much persuasion, he did show me how it was done and I would like to share the secret with you. It's simple but great fun.

You must hold the match that you rub in a special way. Pinch it between thumb and forefinger about three quarters of the way along the match. The fingernail of the second finger is under the very end of the match.

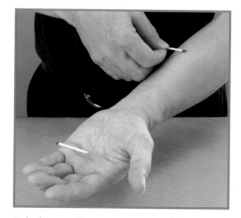

Rub the match on your arm and then, as you bring the two heads together, act as if they are trying to repel each other.

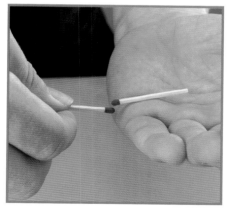

For just a split second bring the head of the rubbed match under the head of the other and...

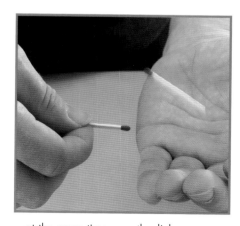

...at the same time secretly click your fingernail on the end of the match. This will cause a minute and unnoticeable seesaw action and the heads will hit one another, causing the other match to jump into the air.

Tips

• Don't dismiss this one for its simplicity because it can get a great reaction.
• Present it as a scientific demonstration of anti-magnetism (whatever that is) rather than as a magic trick.
• The click sound of the fingernail adds to the illusion as it sounds a little like the noise of an electric spark. In fact, I have often found that this can make people jump as high as the match.

Safety warning

• Please only use safety matches for this trick. Rubbing on the sleeve associates the effect with static electricity in people's minds and therefore, in my opinion, strengthens the effect. If you are worried about this, then don't rub the match, blow on it instead. Be sensible with matches at all times and keep them in a safe, dry place away from children and animals.

Coins and Cards

Moves and Flourishes

BEFORE HEADING into this section of card tricks, it is useful to know a few moves, terms and flourishes. Hundreds of books have been written on card magic alone and the serious and advanced student will search these out. You will not need sleights for all of the effects but with these in your magical 'armoury' you will soon be developing your own routines.

Pack face down
The 'top' of the deck will normally mean the top card of a face-down pack.

Pack face up
The card that you can see is referred to as the face card or bottom card in the deck.

The fan
This is shown face down.

Ribbon spread

This can also be done with the cards face up. It is a neat way of showing all the cards to the audience at the table and if you place your fingers under the bottom card (far right in the photograph), and flip it over, all the other cards will turn over as well.

Holding a 'break' in the pack

The size of the break is exaggerated for clarity and should not be discernible from the front.

The glide

This is a worm's eye view. With this you can take cards from the (apparent) bottom of the pack without changing the bottom card.

The double lift

Taking two cards as if they were one.

The overhand shuffle

The most common and easiest shuffle.

The riffle shuffle

Practise until it looks easy and natural.

False overhand shuffle

A false shuffle is one that maintains one or more cards in a known position or order. For our purposes we will assume that you want to keep track of the top card during an overhand shuffle. I have marked the card with a cross for clarity in the photographs. I wouldn't suggest that you do this in real life unless you are doing card tricks for an extremely shortsighted mole.

Tip

• In a similar way to the false overhand shuffle, you could also get a secret glimpse of the bottom/face card and then shuffle it to the top. No need then to know beforehand what the top card is, if you are using a borrowed deck.

Begin the shuffle by ensuring that at least the first card is run off singly.

Continue shuffling off the rest of the pack in a mix of singles and multiples. Your known card will now be at the bottom.

Repeat the shuffle making sure that at least the last one or two cards are shuffled off singly. Your known card will now be back on top.

Card Forcing

THE BASIC PREMISE for many card tricks is that the spectator chooses a card and then the magician discovers which card it is. OK, it sounds very boring written like that or performed like that, but there is huge scope for entertainment to be woven into the effect. So wouldn't it make your conjuring career a lot easier if you knew exactly which card the spectator was going to choose before the trick began?

This is what is called forcing a card onto a spectator, while giving them the impression that they have a perfectly free choice. You have to know the position and value of a card before you start. Usually this is the top card, occasionally the bottom. You already know, from the previous section, how to control your known card to the top or bottom during a shuffle.

Again, the large cross on the card is only for clarity in the pictures!

Cross-cut force

The force card is on top. Ask a spectator to cut the pack wherever they like...

...making two piles

You pick up the bottom half and put it crossways on top the other. Now you need to create some 'time misdirection' so look at the spectator and mention the impossibility of you knowing exactly where she would cut the pack.

Turn back to the pack and pick up the upper half. Point to the top card of the lower half and ask them to pick up the card that they cut to but not show it to you.

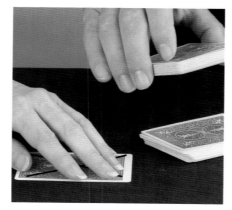

They will take the card and keep it close to their chest. They will have no idea that you already know what it is!

Tip

• The moves in this force are beautifully choreographed to confuse the spectator. They will really believe that they cut to that card. Now you can read their mind or let them shuffle the card back into the pack. Either way, you know what the card is so you can relax and have some fun!

Out-of-sight force

This force is all done underneath a large handkerchief on the assumption that neither you nor the spectator can see which card is being chosen. Well, that is what they think! Again the force card starts out on top.

If the handkerchief was in all the photos you really wouldn't see much, so after the first step, we have swapped it for a length of ribbon for clarity.

Remember that it has to be a large opaque handkerchief in real life!

The spectator is asked to reach under the handkerchief to take a card.

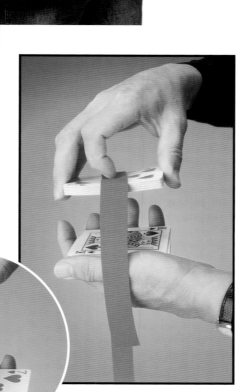

As you put the pack underneath the handkerchief, you secretly turn it face up.

Now dribble the cards into your other hand until the spectator says stop.

Before the spectator reaches underneath to take their selection, secretly turn all the cards in your left hand over.

Drop the rest of the cards onto the ones in your left hand, turning them face down as you do so. You can now remove the handkerchief, as you are home and dry.

They will now take the original top card or force card.

Slip-cut force

Riffle through the cards using your thumb until the spectator says stop.

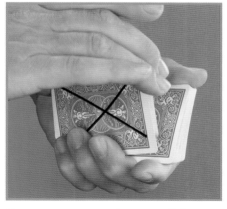

You now appear to take away all the cards above this point. In fact, see how my left fingers are keeping a friction grip on the top card.

Move the discarded cards towards the spectator while you say something to them to catch their attention.

Now point back at the cards in your left hand and ask them to take the card they stopped you at. It is of course, the force card held back by your fingers

Performance notes

• Practise this force over and over until you can execute it really smoothly.

• You might be asking yourself by now, why on earth do you need another forcing method? Well, you will often wish to have more than one card chosen or do several card tricks in your show and you should not repeat the same force any more than you should repeat a trick.

Palming

THIS IS A very useful sleight for removing the top card from a pack. You may just want it out of the way or you may want to find it in a completely different place at the conclusion of the trick.

Performance notes
• Obviously it is necessary that you provide some degree of misdirection to the spectators while you perform this move or it will be obvious what you are doing.

You have already controlled the card on to the top of the pack.

Briefly cover the card with your flat hand and push it a few millimetres away from yourself.

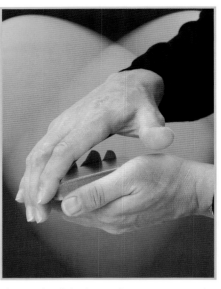

The card will be levered up into your palm.

Curl the hand just a fraction in order to be able to grip the card and lift it away.

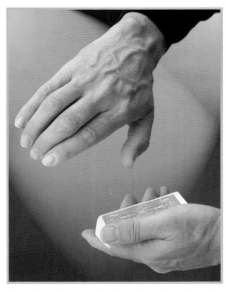

Your hand conceals the palmed card and you can continue performing the trick.

What the audience cannot see.

Out of a Scrape

YOU COULD be in a bit of a scrape if somebody pushed an old pack of cards at you and said, 'Show us a trick'.

This works particularly well with an old pack such as a family pack. A family pack is one where the four of spades is stained yellow where the baby was sick over it, the seven of diamonds is missing the corner that the puppy ate, the jack of clubs has been made out of part of a breakfast cereal box as no one knows where it is (but everyone suspects that Aunt Maud threw it on the fire last Christmas) and the rest of the pack looks like it has been left out in the garden for a week – because it has.

Have a card chosen in the usual manner. Get the spectator to look at the card, show it to their friends and remember it.

Allow the spectator to push it back in but grip the fan tightly so that they cannot return it all the way.

Go to push it in the rest of the way yourself but, as you do so, use your fingernail to scrape the edge of the card.

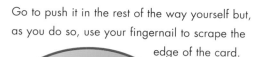

Close the fan and the whiter scrape mark can clearly be seen.

Don't let anyone see you looking for the mark though or you will give the game away.

Tips
• If you find it hard to get to the scraped card without it looking very obvious what you are doing, then you could turn your back while you search. Be quick though or you might turn around again and find the audience has disappeared.
• After you have made the scrape mark, you can immediately hand out the cards for them to be shuffled again as it is very unlikely that this will make it harder for you to detect it.

Circus Card Trick

THIS IS A classic among card tricks and I include it here for that reason and also as a demonstration of the 'key card' principle. The trick is reputed to have been a scam used by roustabouts in travelling fairs to fleece punters of a few quid. I trust that you will be using this effect for its entertainment value only!

First, what is a key card?

Secretly glimpse the bottom card before or during the process of having a card chosen. This will be the key card. Here it is the ace of hearts.

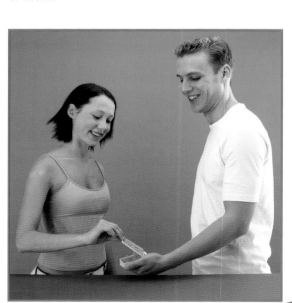

Ask the spectator to replace the chosen card on the top of the deck and then cut the pack to lose the selection somewhere in the middle.

Cut it again and then let the spectator cut the pack a few more times.

Notes

• It does not matter how many single cuts a spectator does – the key card sequence will not be disturbed.

• If in the process of the cuts the key card ends up back at the bottom, the selection will then be on the top.

Look through the pack and the selection will be the card immediately to the right of the key card. This is the key card principle and it is used in a number of tricks.

For the *Circus Card Trick*, continue as follows:

Hold the deck face down and deal from the top, turning each card face up onto the table as you go.

Pretend to feel for magic vibrations coming from the cards.

When you see the key card, do not react but carry on dealing for another five or six cards.

Suddenly you feel a sensation and claim that you are sure that the next card that you are going to turn over is the right one. In fact, you are so sure that you are prepared to gamble the next round of drinks on it.

Tip
• Wherever possible get the spectator who chose the card to show it to a friend. This helps to prevent the spectator from forgetting her card or trying to change her mind in order to mess up your trick. This applies to most card tricks, not just this one.

Knowing that you have gone way past her card, she will definitely take you up on that. So you reach over and turn her card face down! Don't wait for the drink, just run!

The Coin Speaks?

IF YOU asked a friend to hide a coin in one of his hands, could you tell for certain which hand it was in? If you follow this simple routine, the answer is yes.

To start with you turn your back, so that you cannot see anything that your friend is doing.

Ask your friend to put the coin in one hand. He may change hands several times if he wishes, but he must tell you when he has come to a final decision.

Now ask him to hold the coin in his hand against his ear and listen hard. You tell him that he may or may not be able to hear anything but it does not matter, as it is you who will pick up the signals later.

When you are satisfied that he has heard enough, tell him to put both hands in front of him, then you turn around. Glance quickly at his hands.

Now look deep into his eyes and hold your hand close to his ears to pick up the signals.

You point to one hand, then the other and finally decide on your choice. When he opens his hand there is the coin. You must have picked up strange vibrations from him…

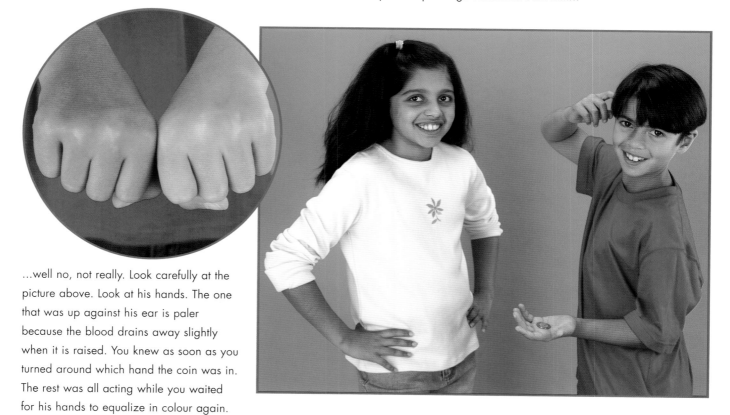

…well no, not really. Look carefully at the picture above. Look at his hands. The one that was up against his ear is paler because the blood drains away slightly when it is raised. You knew as soon as you turned around which hand the coin was in. The rest was all acting while you waited for his hands to equalize in colour again.

After all, you do not want him to look straight down and realize the difference himself. He might think you are cheating!

Tip

• You don't have to use a coin – any small object that will fit neatly in a hand will work. If you want to be like a wizard, you could find some bizarre little ornament and pretend it has mystical powers.

Lazy Card Trick

SOMETIMES IT is good to let the spectator appear to do the magic, as you do not want the audience to feel you are always getting the better of them. Here, have a card chosen and discover for yourself which card it was without letting on to the audience that you know. You could either force a card (see Card Forcing page 95) or, even better, use the 'key card' principle (see Circus Card Trick page 100).

Tips

• I strongly advise you not to do this more than once or twice or you will almost certainly get found out.

• You will probably realize once you have practised that you could use this same method for forcing the bottom card.

Now feign difficulty in finding their card as you search through the pack. Contrive secretly to get the card to the bottom of the pack as you do this. Now you say something like 'I really feel too lazy to find your card. Would you find it for me?'

As you say this, start to pull back cards with your right forefinger as shown. Ask the spectator to tell you when to stop.

What the spectator can't see is that your right thumb is under the bottom card, which is, of course, their chosen card.

When they say stop, begin to lift all the cards above that point. In the photo, we have exposed that action so that you can see that the thumb is pulling the bottom card up with the top group of cards.

Ask them to name their card and then lift up the top portion so that they can see that they stopped at the right card. Also notice in the photo, how it is just possible for you to glimpse the new bottom card at the same time by tilting the cards slightly in your left hand.

Congratulate them on their accuracy and ask them if, while they are about it, could they please find another card for you, as you will need it tomorrow. Repeat the process, naming the card glimpsed.

Congratulate them yet again and ask the rest of the audience to give them a round of applause.

The Coin Safe That Isn't

PERHAPS IN your act you have
already done some coin
vanishes with a coin borrowed from
a spectator. They will therefore be
relieved when you offer to wrap that
item of hard-earned cash in a
handkerchief for safety and to let
them hold it. Safety? They don't
know much about your magic then,
do they? Even though they are
holding the handkerchief, which is
twisted tightly around the coin, you
still manage to produce it from
behind an ear. No, not your
ear…theirs!

You just need two things

• A coin – a larger size is better
visually and easier to manipulate,
and it is much more fun if you
have borrowed it from a spectator.
At least they will be
watching you closely.
• A handkerchief –
a medium size silk
one would be best
but, whatever else,
it must be clean!

Display the coin
between thumb
and forefinger.

Spread the
handkerchief
over the coin
and your
hand.

As you apparently straighten the coin with your other hand, you pinch a little cloth behind the coin with your thumb.

Lift the front of the handkerchief once more to 'prove' that it is still there.

With a flick of the wrist the handkerchief is tossed forward. The key thing here is that the whole handkerchief now drapes over the front of your hand. Earlier it was just the front half.

Twist the bulk of the handkerchief below the coin. The shape of the coin is clearly visible.

Here is a magician's view below the coin – you can see the real situation.

The spectator pinches the twist in his fingers to make sure that the coin cannot escape.

As you get him to cover the coin with the palm of his other hand, let the coin slip from the gap in the cloth into your own fingers.

Now simply reach behind his ear and pretend to produce the coin from there.

Tip

• Remember that impromptu means not planned in advance. It definitely does not mean unprepared. To make an impromptu trick look natural and spur-of-the-moment, it should be extremely well rehearsed.

Balancing a Coin by Your Fingertips

A QUICKIE THAT purports to demonstrate your skill with coins. This could be included amongst some other coin routines. You will have already shown some coin magic so now you demonstrate your 'coin control'.

The coin is picked up with a pin already hidden behind it.

As you place the coin by your fingertips, slide the pinhead between them.

Hey presto! What skill!

Tips

• Feign a little difficulty in performing this feat at first. It will make it seem harder and thus more skilful.

• When you have finished this effect, take the coin from your fingertips with the other hand and pass it out to a spectator for examination or for them to try it for themselves. Let the 'balancing hand' fall naturally to your side so that you can allow the pin to drop unnoticed onto your magic table.

Don't let it fall on the floor and then tread on it or you will be performing another type of balancing act as you hop around on one foot. Ouch!

Remember to take care with sharp objects

Flipping Card

W**HEN I AM** performing my magic professionally, many people ask me how I do it or if I could teach them a trick. Naturally, due to the rules of The Magic Circle, I cannot tell them but, occasionally, I meet someone who has a genuine interest in magic rather than just wanting to find out how everything is done. If I can determine that they are an amateur or hobby magician, then this is the trick that I will teach them. As you have shown a genuine interest by purchasing this book devoted entirely to magic, I will teach it to you too.

Shuffle the cards or ask a spectator to do so. Fan them out, face down, and ask him to choose a card.

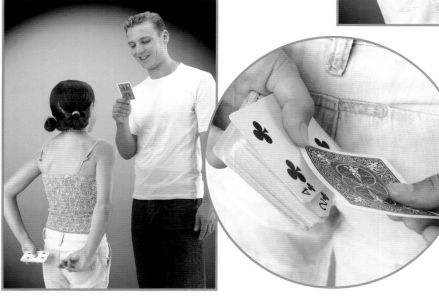

Mention to your spectator that your skill is such that you can now do card tricks behind your back. As you say this put the pack behind your back and turn it face up.

Now turn the top card face down and bring the pack round to the front again. All this happens in an instant and the pack will still look the same. In fact, all the cards are face up except the top one.

Keeping the pack squared up, have the spectator return the card somewhere in the middle of the pack.

Now put the whole pack behind your back again while you attempt to find the chosen card. Pull off the reversed top card and show it to the spectator. It's wrong. (But then you knew that.)

Meanwhile, turn the whole pack face down behind your back and show him one or two more cards off the top. He will say 'wrong again', so look a little crestfallen and say that you will have to try some advanced magic.

Bring the face-down pack around to the front and mime taking an invisible card from the pack, turning it face up and pushing it back in the pack. Claim that you have turned his chosen card over.

Fan out all the cards, face up. One card is seen to be face down. Ask the spectator to name his card. He does.

It is the correct one.

Tips

• When the chosen card is pushed back into the deck, keep a finger at your end of the pack to ensure that no face-up cards are pushed out. This would definitely give the game away.

• When you fan out all the cards at the end you could, of course, fan them face down and show the face-up card right away. The way I have shown it, though, builds to a better and more magical climax.

The French Drop

THIS IS probably the first coin-vanish that aspiring magicians will learn. However, although easy to master, it does take some care and attention to detail to make it look convincing. This, then, is not only a good effect but also a good lesson in making your moves appear natural.

The premise is that you show a coin, take it into your hand and then cause it to vanish.

The first two elements are all important to you, but should be of no, I repeat no, significance to your spectator. But you need to carry out these actions, so invent a reason for doing them. This way they will not look like magician's moves even if they are. All the magic must appear to happen at stage three.

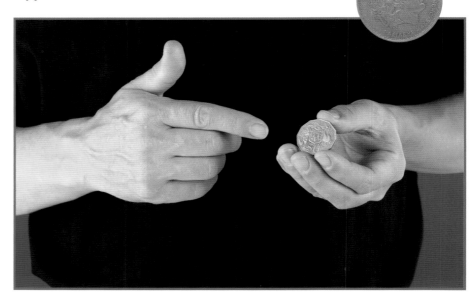

You are showing a coin to your audience. Think 'Why?' So make an appropriate comment about the coin – its date, its wear and tear, or its value.

Take it in your other hand. Again, think 'Why?' So you can hold it nearer to the spectator perhaps, or so you can hold it in your right hand to get your wand out of your pocket with your left.

Wave your magic wand, sprinkle your 'woofle dust', ask your spectator to give a magic blow, say a magic spell, or do whatever suits your magic style.

Open your hand. The coin has vanished.

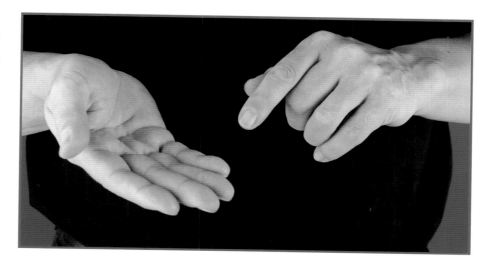

Tip
Practise this by first taking the coin for real. Now do the French Drop. The two actions should look identical

So where did it go?

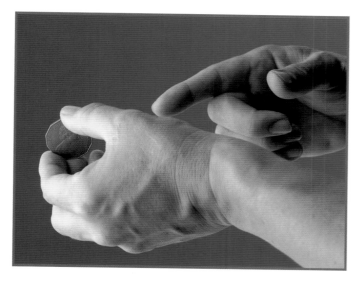

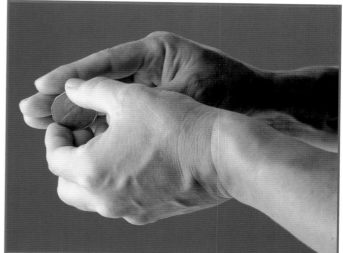

As you go to take the coin in the right hand, simply open your left fingers just a fraction and the coin will fall down behind them. The right hand continues as if it has grasped the coin and moves away to the right.

As it does this, the left hand must freeze for a moment with a coin-sized empty space at the fingertips where it was last seen. The spectator's eyes will follow the moving right hand.

Only now can the left hand move.

It could reach into your pocket for a wand and get rid of the coin or you can reach forward and pluck the coin from behind your spectator's ear. The choice is yours.

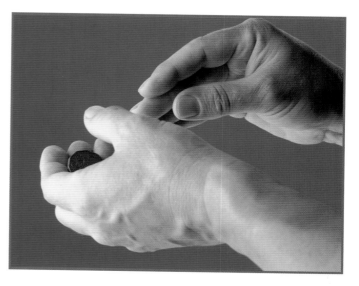

Cardflick

TWO NAMED cards are pulled from the centre of the pack in a split second with just a flick of the wrist. This is a famous card trick that spectators, both adults and children, often ask to show me after one of my performances. It's easy, but it is so often done badly. Let's hope this method will help you all to perform it with the care that it deserves.

Here is what it should look like. You borrow a pack of cards, check through it, remove two cards, show them to your spectators and replace them in two different places near the centre of the pack. This is how 'the speed of the hand deceives the eye'. Toss the cards from one hand to the other with a flick of the wrist and, with lightning speed, pull out the same two cards and show them to your gob-smacked audience.

The secret?

They are not the same two cards, but they certainly appear to be.

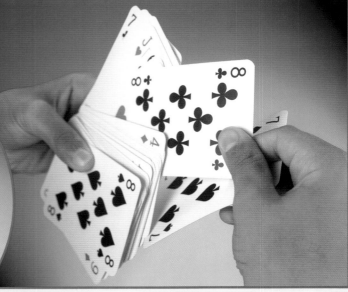

You apparently check, shuffle and cut the cards. Actually you arrange to get two cards of same colour, different suit and consecutive numbers onto the top and bottom of the pack.

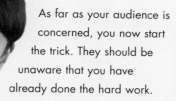

As far as your audience is concerned, you now start the trick. They should be unaware that you have already done the hard work.

Pull out your two favourite cards of the day. (Actually the look-alikes of the other two.) Show them briefly to the audience, calling them 'a black seven and a black eight'. (Do not mention the suits.)

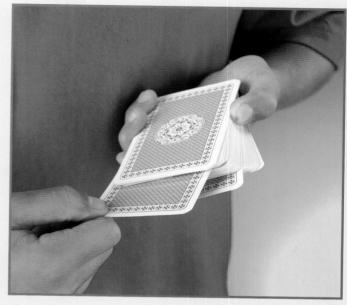

Place them fairly and squarely into the middle portion of the pack. Now do your little chat about the quickness of the hand.

As you flick the cards towards your other hand, the friction of your fingers will easily retain the top and bottom cards. It all happens so quickly. Display the cards.

The audience will be convinced that they are seeing the same cards as earlier.

You must be a sleight of hand expert, so practise hard.

Tips

• Arrange the cards while you say that you are checking to see if the pack is complete or if there are any jokers. There is no need to turn your back on the audience and fiddle around out of sight. This is a common mistake and it looks awful.

• Do not forget the bit of chat about 'the speed of the hand deceives the eye'. Magicians call this 'time misdirection'. It takes the audience's mind off the cards for a moment or two, so that they will not so easily be able to remember and differentiate between the cards they saw at the start and those that you finally produce.

• Use mid to high numbered spot cards such as sevens, eights, nines or court cards. They are more confusing to the eye.

Coin Scone

THERE IS a very old gag whereby you offer to turn a coin into a cake. You make it vanish and say 'Look - scone!' If you use this terrible gag, I cannot guarantee that your audience will not decide to form a lynch mob and revive that ancient tradition of burning witches and magicians. So, how about a really easy and clean coin vanish? Will you need magic powers? No, just barefaced cheek.

The scenario

Take some change out of your pocket and ask someone to point to a coin.

Take that coin and put the rest of the change back in your pocket.

Rub the coin into the palm of your hand.

Show your palm is now empty. The audience are naturally suspicious of your other fingers.

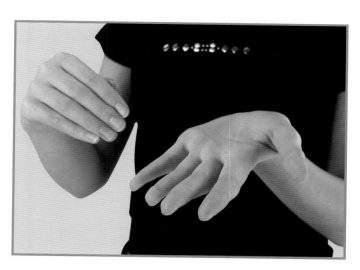

Now show all your fingers are empty. Wow!

Look again at stage two. Our magician never actually took the coin but simply pushed it out of sight beneath the others and returned them all to her pocket.

You must believe that you have a coin in your fingers. If you believe it yourself then the audience will not question it. Study how your fingers look when they do hold a coin and copy it. Be confident and look only at the audience or your other hand. Believe me, afterwards they will want to check up your sleeves and under your fingernails. They just will not think that you could have been so brazen as never to have never taken the coin at all.

Performance notes

• The two photographs at the top of this page show another form of misdirection. Making the fingers look a bit awkward and suspicious diverts the audience's attention away from the real method for a moment. It is then far more difficult for them to backtrack in their minds to the point at which you did the 'tricky business'. There is a lot of psychology in magic.

Tips

• You ideally need to take a coin from the middle or bottom of the pile so if they choose a top coin, then give them a stir with your fingers as you say, 'Are you sure?' Even easier, choose the coin yourself!
• I would not suggest that you try this as your only coin trick. Once you have shown that you can do magic with coins or whatever, then try this one. Spectators will be looking to see what sleight of hand you are using and will be baffled as you will not actually be using any!

Great Minds Think Alike

YOU AND a spectator have a deck of cards each. You shuffle each other's decks then both choose a card from your own deck. Now you turn that card upside down in his deck and he turns his card upside down in yours. When you compare the cards they match. Coincidence or magic?

Definitely magic and, although well disguised, it uses the key card principle.

Here's how

Throughout this trick you should both try to mirror each other's actions.

Swap decks, shuffle and return them. Secretly note the bottom card of their deck before you return it.

Each take a card from somewhere in the pack...

...look at it, remember it and put it on the top of the pack. (In fact, don't bother to remember your own card – you won't need it.)

Now cut your packs to lose the card somewhere in the middle.

Then swap packs again. You state that you should each find the card you remembered and turn it upside down in the pack. In fact, because you know the key card and the key card principle (see Circus Card Trick page 100), you will actually find HIS remembered card and turn THAT one upside down. He, of course will be finding the same card in the pack he is holding.

Return the packs again and both spread them out, face up, in front of you. One card in each should be face down.

On the count of three, both turn the face-down card face up.

They match! Great minds really must think alike.

Tips

- Just to remind you, his card will be the one immediately to the right of the key card, when you fan the cards face up.
- Because of the shuffling and swapping the packs back and forth, even if someone knew of the key card principle, they would never guess that you could be using it here.

Coin Through The Hand

PEOPLE SOMETIMES ask a magician, 'Have you got special hands?' They will often ask to inspect your hands – I imagine it is to see if you have had special trapdoors fitted!

Here is a very simple coin trick to play along with these notions. You could explain that you have an invisible coin slot through your hand. Borrow a coin and demonstrate.

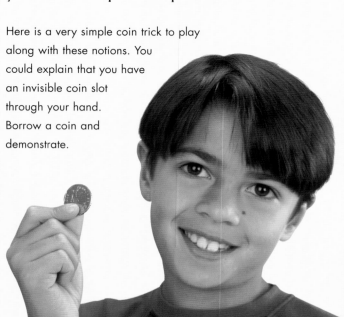

Hold the coin above your clenched fist and offer to show how you can push a coin through the back of your hand.

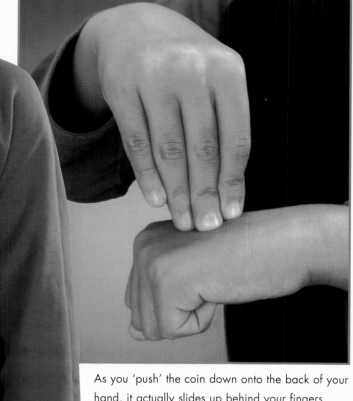

As you 'push' the coin down onto the back of your hand, it actually slides up behind your fingers.

Open your hand with great aplomb to show the coin. 'Oops, it must have got stuck.' OK, so you have not fooled anyone – yet.

Now, as you turn your hand back into a fist, you do the 'move'. As your thumb virtually brushes against the tips of your fingers holding the coin, you let it go.

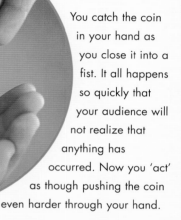

You catch the coin in your hand as you close it into a fist. It all happens so quickly that your audience will not realize that anything has occurred. Now you 'act' as though pushing the coin even harder through your hand.

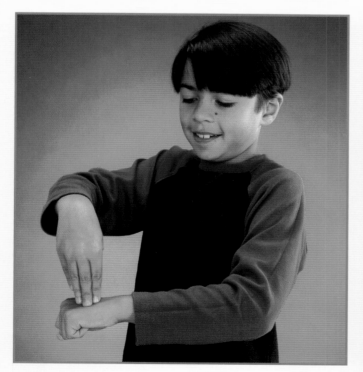

'I will have to push harder.'

Tip

• Use a fairly large and heavy coin. It will fall from the fingers more quickly without sticking.

Slowly open your fist to reveal the coin. Just when the audience thought that they had caught you, you caught them!

Clipped!

WOULDN'T IT be great to be able to shuffle a pack of cards, get several people to choose a card each, shuffle each one back into the pack, and yet be able to find their cards, without even looking. Just by feel. Sleight of hand with cards can take many years to learn and even more years to perfect, so here is a little 'cheat' method to get you doing amazing card magic almost straight away. You just need an assistant. But this one won't ask for wages or fancy costumes because your assistant will be... a paperclip!

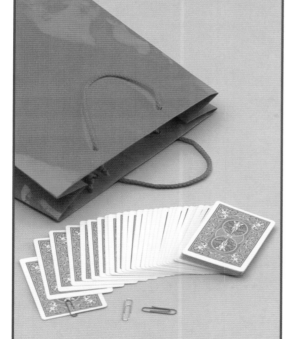

The effect

You are going to be able to select the cards chosen by each of your audience simply by 'feel'.

Tips

• Try to use a flat paperclip with no lip, as this will cause a less obvious 'break' in the pack.

• When cutting the cards keep them tilted slightly towards yourself, so that the audience cannot see the clip.

• There is always a very, very slim chance that someone will try to choose the bottom card with the clip. A way around this would be to start off with two cards in the clip. If they did take a card from the bottom then it is no problem as you are still left with a clipped card. You can either slip one of the cards out during your final shuffle or simply leave them both there. As long as you remember that you clipped two cards it won't affect the trick.

• When feeling for the cards you can take a little time 'acting' as if it were an incredibly difficult task.

• The magic would seem even stronger if you borrowed a pack of cards for this trick. Simply secretly slip a paperclip on while you are 'checking the cards'.

The paperclip is on the bottom card on the short edge nearest you. Keep the shorter loop of the clip on top (the back) of the card.

Shuffle the cards. Practise this and you will find it very easy to 'control' the clipped card to the top or bottom of the pack. You can easily feel it with your thumb.

Offer the top and middle of the pack to each of the spectators keeping the clipped card hidden well below.

Cut the cards in your hands. Feel for the clip with your thumb then cut all the cards above it to the bottom.

Take back the cards. They go, one at a time, onto the top of the pack sliding into the clip which is concealed under your thumb.

Shuffle and cut – as before – between each card being returned. Give the pack a final shuffle and drop it into a bag or box.

The spectator gives the bag a final shake to mix up the cards.

Gently feel for the cards which are clipped together. Turn them so that the short side of the clip is on top.

Bring out the top card. This will be the last one chosen, so you know whose card it is. Likewise all the others will still be in the order that they were chosen, so you can give the right card to the right person.

Coin Karate

A SIMPLE BUT effective transformation trick. A 10p coin is borrowed and placed inside a folded piece of paper. You put this in your palm and karate-chop it with your other hand. When you unfold the packet you find two 5p coins. If the karate chop makes all your fingers fall off, you are probably hitting too hard.

Preparation

A second identical piece of paper is folded, with two 5p coins inside, and glued to the middle of the other. This is your secret gimmick.

The performance

Borrow a 10p coin and ask if anyone ever has a problem finding the right small change.

Tips

• Any coins could be used as long as the value of the two smaller ones adds up to the value of the larger one. Small and light coins are better.

• Put a little dab of soap between the coins in their packet. This will help to prevent them moving and 'talking'. 'Talking' is a magician's term describing when hidden objects make a noise and give the game away.

• Use good quality notepaper or art paper that is thick enough for the hidden packet not to be detected. Lightly pre-crease the paper so that both will fold in exactly the same place.

Bring the paper from your pocket, taking care not to show the gimmick.

Place the 10p coin in the middle.

Fold the paper as shown. The curve of your palm will keep the gimmick hidden.

Turn the packet over as you bring it up to your mouth to give it a magic blow.

Do the karate chop...

...and unfold the paper.

Give the 5p coins to your volunteer, then crumple up the paper, as if it were empty, and put it in your pocket.

Tips
• The action of turning the packet over is disguised by the larger motion of bringing it up to your mouth. Often in magic, you will find that you can hide a small movement within a large one.

• Finally keep a spare 10p in your pocket for two reasons. Firstly, no one in the audience may have a 10p coin for your trick and, secondly, if someone does lend you one, they might just object to getting two 5p coins in return. Be prepared.

Calculating Cuts

THIS COULD be a good effect for the office. You may have noticed that some display numbers on many calculators read as letters when the calculator is held upside down. Type **0.7734** into yours, turn it upside down and it should appear to say the word **HELLO**. If yours does this, then you can try the following trick. You will also need a pack of cards.

Explain to your spectator that numbers can often be read as letters on your calculator and, while talking, type in a few numbers. Discuss numerology and the significance of certain numbers, asking him for some as you proceed. Age, shoe size, date of birth, whatever. They are not important, as you will secretly contrive to make the calculator read 0.7734 and declare that by the 'power of numerology' you have a message for him. Show him the HELLO. OK, this is not a side-splitting gag but it sets you up for the magic to follow.

Now type in some more numbers, as if doing a very complicated sum. Finish with the display reading 45. Place the calculator to one side, upside down and so that the spectator cannot see the display. Claim by the special numerological powers that you possess, you have made a prediction of the future and bring out your playing cards.

Performance notes

• You will see that 45 can read as 4s (4 of spades) or upside down as 5h (5 of hearts). This is the basis of this trick.

• In this trick, you will also learn to riffle shuffle without disturbing the top or bottom card and about the 'Magician's Choice'.

• Showing the upside-down calculator at the end of the trick will seem quite natural, because you did the HELLO gag at the beginning. Showing it the right way up will also seem perfectly natural as you talked about numbers looking like letters earlier.

You have previously put the five of hearts and the four of spades at the top and bottom of the pack. It doesn't matter which is on top, as long as you remember.

Cut the pack into two halves. Riffle the two halves together making sure that your thumbs release the original bottom card(s) first and the top card(s) last. This will leave the top and bottom card as before. Practise this.

Cut the pack again and ask the spectator to think carefully and then to discard one half or the other. She can even change her mind if she likes. You will now have a half pack with either a prediction card on the top or on the bottom. As you saw which pile she discarded, you will know which is the case.

Now learn the Magician's Choice moves. This is a really useful strategy whereby the spectator seems to make all the choices, but you always end up with the situation that you wanted. You can use this in all kinds of magic, not just with cards. Note that the 'special' pile has been circled in white, just so that you can follow it in the photographs.

Ask her to deal the remaining cards into three piles. Keep your eye on where your predicted card ends up. This is very easy as it will be either the first or the last card dealt.

Ask her to place her hands over two of the piles. If she happens to put her hands on the two piles without the 5h or 4s (above left), then ask her to discard both of those piles. You can then move straight to the last stage. Alternatively she will have her hands on the special pile and one other (above right). You then discard the pile she has not covered and ask her to push one of the piles under her hands towards you.

If she pushes the special pile towards you, then get her to discard the other. If she pushes the other pile towards you, then you discard that one and ask her to keep the other.

Now ask her to turn the top card of the pile over or turn the whole pile over. You will know which. Remind her that she has discarded most of the pack to end up with one card. Show her the calculator display, keeping it upside down if necessary for 5h, or naturally turning it the right way round for 4s. Your numerological prophecy was correct!

Tip
• During the Magician's Choice, it must always seem that whichever course the spectator chooses, your next move was the one that you always intended to make. Her choices must seem to have no bearing on your moves. Then the whole sequence will appear completely fair. A fair magic move? That has to be an oxymoron.

Betcha's

A 'BETCHA' TRICK is one where you might state 'I betcha (bet you) can't do this' and then go on to demonstrate an impossible trick.

Cash on Tap

Offer someone £20 if they can tap the table a dozen times. Most people would jump at the chance to have a go. This can be done on a vertical surface such as a wall or on a table. Ask the participant to hold your note under the knuckle of her middle finger as shown. If on the wall, she must not let the note drop. If on the tabletop, she must not let you pull it away.

Now she must tap three times with her thumb. Still she must not lift her knuckle.

Then three times with her little finger.

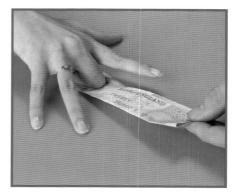

Then three times with her forefinger. And finally three times with her ring finger.

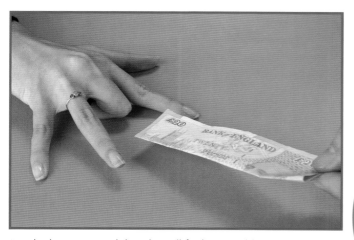

It is the last command that she will find impossible to do without lifting her knuckle and thereby letting the note go. Try it yourself to check that it really does work before you bet your money. This trick can also be performed using a coin.

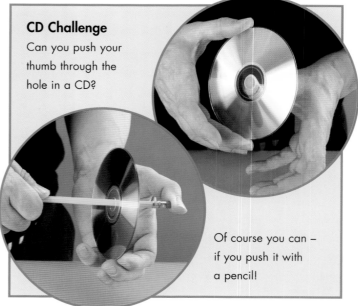

CD Challenge

Can you push your thumb through the hole in a CD?

Of course you can – if you push it with a pencil!